MANAGING UPWARDS

MANAGING UPWARDS

JONATHAN COATES

Gower

Published by
Gower Publishing Limited
Gower House
Croft Road
Aldershot
Hampshire GU11 3HR
England

Gower
Old Post Road
Brookfield
Vermont 05036
USA

HD
38
.C565
1994

British Library Cataloguing in Publication Data
Coates, Jonathan
  Managing Upwards
  I. Title
  658

ISBN 0–566–07485–0

Library of Congress Cataloging-in-Publication Data
Coates, Jonathan.
  Managing upwards/Jonathan Coates.
    p. cm.
  Includes bibliographical references and index.
  ISBN 0–566–07485–0
  1. Management. 2. Organizational change. I. Title.
HD38.C565 1994   94–173
658.4–dc20   CIP

Typeset in Garamond and Avant Garde by Bournemouth Colour Graphics, Parkstone, Dorset and printed in Great Britain at the University Press, Cambridge.

CONTENTS

LIST OF FIGURES

PREFACE

❖

Most of the ideas for *Managing Upwards* have come from my work, over many years, in consulting and training. I have seen the need for it. I have seen it working and I have seen it not working. The many illustrations used in this book come from real organizations and from real people working in organizations but all the names have been changed.

This is not intended to be an academic textbook, read from cover to cover. It offers a basis of experience from which to work, to test theories and to give the reader an opportunity to identify with actual situations. I hope that it will be read and enjoyed by managers of all kinds in all sorts of organizations.

Readers can roam around the chapters as they wish but the two final chapters will require a different approach. These chapters are designed for those who wish to change to a more upward style of management. They look carefully at how to acquire the skills needed to succeed and readers will find practice essential here.

Jonathan Coates

ACKNOWLEDGEMENTS

❖

I first began to work out some ideas about *Managing Upwards* about five years ago. There is very little written about it explicitly and so I set out to put some ideas on paper. The other books that I have written have all flowed together quite quickly; this one seems to have taken forever. The consequence of this is that many people have generally suffered from my ceaseless stop-go progress.

I have to thank my friend and co-director in the Centre for Action Learning Ltd, Claire Breeze, for constantly persuading me that there was a book in it. And I have to thank Margaret Bone who typed draft after draft and would then nag me to produce more and more copy. Special thanks to Dodie Craik who said to me 'if you ever write a good book you ought to get someone to edit it so the others will be able to read it'. She edited the manuscript and constantly questioned me about the meaning I intended to convey.

Finally I have to thank Alison and my family for putting up with endless excuses about 'just finishing off the chapter'. And especial thanks to Rachel and Tom, my children, and Bella too, who taught me what upward management was really about. 'Dad, that's not much of an idea. It would be better if we did it this way.'

JC

1

WHAT IS MANAGING UPWARDS?

Browse through the shelves of any large bookshop that specializes in management or business books and you will find a number of books with titles such as 'How to Manage Your Boss'. There is something odd about such a title: perhaps it is the use of the word 'Boss'. These books will show you how to get your own way by such tactics as making the boss think that your good idea was originally their good idea. They tell you how to manipulate in a very subtle way.

Managing upwards is not tricky, manipulative or subversive. It is perfectly normal and open and when used properly adds enormously to the effectiveness of organizations. Managers frequently have a unique opinion of their work; they know their bit of the organization – its strengths and weaknesses – better than anyone else could and are thus in a unique position to do something about it, if only they would.

Branch managers will be far more knowledgeable and aware about their region than managers in head office. Brand managers will know their markets better than the market research department. Often they could take or propose management action from their unique vantage point but they don't. They wait for someone else to do it for them because 'it's their job and not mine'. Because they do not understand managing upwards, they often wait a long time for action which is less effective than that of which they themselves are capable.

Take Michael Pearce, for example; an engineer and senior manager in a construction company, most of his work involves major projects in the petrochemical industries. Michael does not understand about managing upwards. He is frustrated at work by an out-of-date cost control system which was designed and implemented some years ago for housing projects and is not specific enough for his work. He frequently lets management know that this is the case; sometimes in his work reports and sometimes, when he has the chance, by complaining in meetings. Management is aware of the problem.

If only he knew it, or asked, Michael would discover that although management is aware of his problem they also have many other problems which they consider to be more important. Although they recognize that what he says is true, it provides them with an irritation rather than an opportunity.

If Michael knew more about managing upwards he could do much better. He could point out the implications of maintaining this out-of-date system in terms of the time and money it takes constantly to adjust it for his type of work. He could indicate the benefits of doing it differently. He could describe how the new system should work (and he knows this better than anyone else). He could try it out on a pilot basis so that he has some evidence of what it looks like. He could think through one or two other options, rather than the one he prefers, to check that there might not be another way. He could then arrange a presentation to management where he can skilfully make his case and ask for approval to try it out on his next project. Or maybe he cannot do all that himself because of lack of expertise. In which case he seeks out help from the accountants or the systems analysts, convinces them of his need and builds their ideas into his proposed action.

Managing upwards is not an appeal to anarchy. Rather it is an attempt to help the whole management process by tapping into all the experience and resources available to provide actionable solutions to problems, rather than complaining and waiting for someone else to do it for you. Sometimes you may well arrive at a situation where you can simply get on with it yourself; sometimes you may have to put it all together in an argued proposal and work hard to influence the outcome.

Kate Jenks does understand managing upwards. She is the warden supervisor of a local authority sheltered home for elderly handicapped people in London, where cuts in local government funds have led to a reduced supply of maintenance materials. Kate cannot operate with her cleaners and maintenance staff in the way that she used to, or the way that she would like. Rather than complain about this or wait for her very busy – and rather difficult – boss to find her a solution, she talked to her staff about the problem. One of them suggested that she went to talk to a similar supervisor in another establishment. In fact she talked to two or three and realized that if they pooled resources (they are all within easy reach) they can spread out the gaps in their supplies and materials. They agreed a three month trial without telling anyone and set up a resource management system. After this they asked the boss to come and see what they had achieved and now the whole council manages its maintenance materials in a pooled way.

Managing upwards doesn't always mean doing things that you imagine management could be doing for you. Sometimes it may mean disagreeing with what they propose for you. Typical examples of this might involve timescales. For example, your boss asks you to do something, which you understand perfectly, by a certain time. Thinking it through you realize that the timescale is not realistic. You have to say so and you have to know the right way to say so. It is unreasonable to scream at the boss, saying things like 'you never think'. It is reasonable, however, to be professional and explain why, in your view, 'Wednesday is too early to complete this work. Thursday would be more reasonable. Does this cause any problems?'.

In my experience of working with managers who give instructions that are seen as unreasonable, the cause is more often carelessness or thoughtlessness on their part rather than malice. Your boss seldom sets out to wreck your work or your life by deliberately issuing unreasonable orders or requests. They, too, are subject to lots of pressures and sometimes they behave unreasonably. Rather than moan and mope, the upward manager asks assertively to check out what the boss had in mind.

This is very important. Accepting a request or an instruction when you know it isn't possible is a lie. Somehow you have to be able to say so and you have to say it without causing offence. Sometimes your work and your experience may lead you to believe there is a better way of carrying out the task. Keeping quiet about it does not add value to the processes of your organization. Of course it depends on 'the way things are round here' and it may be difficult to get a hearing. You will have to work at it but the results are important to you, your boss and your organization.

So that, in brief, is managing upwards. Most managers have managers above them, therefore, managing upwards is a key issue for many managers.

2

MANAGEMENT CULTURE AND INFLUENCE

During a recent stay at a residential training centre, I came across a much photocopied notice in the kitchen area – between the health and safety regulations and the weekend duty roster – which read: 'He may not always be right but he's always the boss.' And underneath, in clear, handwritten letters it said: 'When we let him.' Managers know this from hard experience; sometimes they are allowed to manage and sometimes they are not. This gives us a first clue that management is not a simple downward process but that there might be quite complicated and interesting upward processes that go on at the same time.

Some years ago, in a government department in the United States, I observed an official campaign (in the sense that it was initiated by the human resource department), called 'Prove that your boss's job isn't necessary'. This was a fascinating initiative because it meant that all around the department managers were saying to their bosses 'Let me do that', 'I can do that', 'I'm sure I could do that'. It had the effect of pulling down much of the work that was being accumulated up at the top of the department, leaving senior managers to do important and significant things and, inevitably, leaving one or two senior managers completely stranded. Whilst one aim was to reveal that some senior management was doing far too much middle management work, the main purpose of the exercise was to stimulate putting work into the right place in the organization, with the driving force coming from below.

POWER AND INFLUENCE

In his book *Power and Influence*, John Kotter, from Harvard Business School, writes that management is traditionally viewed as a power downward process. Traditionally, if I am a supervisor I have power over the people I supervise. It is only too obvious to those who supervise just how much power their people have over them. They can use their power in a very subtle way or they can make it very explicit. They can conspire. They can gang up against you. Much management discussion, after work in the pub, concerns people who, in the manager's view, aren't doing what they should do or won't do what they were told to do. It is readily apparent in organizations – and we could include here business, government or even families – that while they may be nominally a manager in charge of other people, the application of this power is not quite as evident as it might be.

Organizations are characterized by their cultures. Cultures, or culture, 'are the things we value here' and there is no doubt that cultures differ from organization to organization. This may be to do with where they are in the world, what they manufacture, how old they are, the style of management and so on. Organizational culture, which is sometimes formalized and sometimes elusive, is simply the accumulation of all the bits and pieces, characters, heroes and villains in the organization. It comes from the history of the organization and often contributes to its success and provides its distinctiveness.

ROLES AND CULTURES IN ORGANIZATIONS

There are a number of ways of discussing and identifying cultures in organizations. One of these is called a 'role culture' where the position of hierarchical superiority on an organization chart says everything. Your organization chart may look a bit like Figure 2.1.

Here we have a manager managing two other managers, who in turn each manage three subordinates, a role culture will say that the top manager in this chart has the most power and the middle managers in this chart have power over the people they manage but are 'in power' to their own manager.

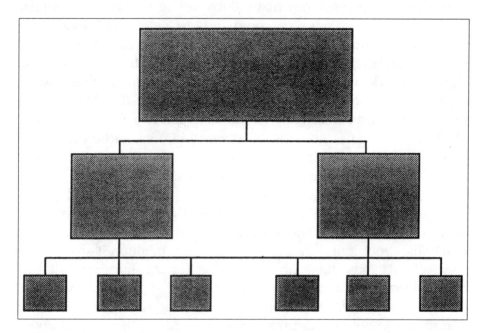

Figure 2.1   A simple hierarchy

The truth is seldom so simple. Even in organizations that manifest role cultures quite strongly – as one imagines government departments or banks – it is no longer sufficient merely to be the person with the notice saying 'Manager' on the door to exercise correctly the power of management. I learned this lesson, though I didn't realize it at the time, when at the age of eleven I was made the captain of the school cricket team. I asked another boy to go to field at a particular position and he said 'No'. I said to him: 'You must go and field over there because I have told you to and I am the captain.' And he said: 'So what!'.

Sometimes role cultures can be embarrassingly uncomfortable when they are obviously not working. One reason for this is that managers can only manage by exercising their role power and have no other basis for influence. Often, sadly, they do not see the need for any basis other than their role. It is important to examine the various other bases for gaining influence over people in formal and informal organizations. There must be alternative ways in which people may influence and gain control of the people who they manage or work with.

Sometimes organizations that exhibit strong role cultures appear to rely heavily on rules or commands to get things done. This would seem natural. Roles define bosses who make the rules. We have a complication about working to the rules. In fact we use the phrase 'working to rule' to imply something restricting in organizational practice. When we say 'they have decided to work to rule', we mean that many of the tasks that we normally expect 'them' to do are not going to be done. When air traffic controllers work to rule there is chaos and airports grind to a halt. When post office staff work to rule, some of our mail is two days late. What is going on if working to the rules means that undertakings go wrong? Organizations have rules that they generally, but not always, apply. They make accommodations. They do deals. They don't talk about it and they say so: 'Let's not mention it shall we?'

All of this must have an implication for the impregnability of role cultures and bring into question the apparently inflexible culture they create. Once you realize that the rules are negotiable you might be able to start managing upwards. If these ideas about organizations and cultures, especially the contrasts between role and power cultures, interest you then you should read Charles Handy's book *Understanding Organizations*.

SOURCES OF POWER IN ORGANIZATIONS

There are seven commonly recognised sources of power in organizations that may lead to influence. These are:

○   role power
○   expert power
○   personal power or charisma
○   reward or sanction power
○   information power
○   network power
○   physical power.

Role power is given to you by your organization and is described by your title – manager, supervisor, team leader. It identifies the name on your door or the name in the box on the organization chart. If your organization is respectful of role power, this may be sufficient on its own.

Expert power comes from your expertise in some or all aspects of your work. People recognize you as an expert either through their own judgement or as a result of being influenced by someone else's judgement. Expert power does not require you to be a Nobel prize winner, just more expert than the others.

It is quite common for these two power bases to exist in two people working together. One has the formal role power; the other has, in the eyes of colleagues, strong expert power. Which power base has the most influence over relationships? It is not hard to see from where conflict and confusion stem.

Personal power or charisma is the third source. The fact that I like her and respect her and admire her values gives her the chance to influence me. Of course, in an ideal world, my formal boss may be valued for his or her expertise and also be someone I personally admire; then there are no confusions about power sources.

These first three power sources are most common and give rise to the most confusion.

Reward or sanction power is when you can influence someone to the extent that you can reward them by promoting them or paying them; or that you could in some way penalize them by taking something away – money, promotion or even the job itself. Civil servants in the UK thinking about managing upwards mention with some apprehension 'the Box 4 marking'. In the general version of the British Civil Service Performance Appraisal scheme a Box 1 mark is for superb performance, way beyond what is expected. Box 3 is satisfactory and Box 4 is less than satisfactory. If your boss has the power to give you a Box 4, in theory he or she can influence your performance.

There is an interesting side issue to reward or sanction power. If the target of the power denies its value then your power base is lost. For instance, if I say to my son: 'Tom, if you'll do the washing up then I'll play cricket with you', I am offering a reward in order to influence him. If, however, he replies:'I've gone off cricket,

Dad', then my influencing approach will fail. Similarly, saying to a worker: 'Do it the way that I say or I'll sack you', will only work if sacking is a threat. If the worker replies: 'Right, I've had enough of working here . . . go on, sack me', then this strategy will also fail.

Information power is the fifth source and it depends on what people know about you or what you know about them. You should not compare this source with expert power. At its most extreme, information power might take the form of blackmail but in organizations you don't have to be so extreme in order to be influential. Keeping information close to your chest is a well-known and traditional power base.

Network power comes from who do you know and whether they will be influential for you. This too has an extreme version called being the son of the boss but this too is rare. The real effect of network power depends on how much time and trouble you take in making 'the right contacts' in the organization . . . and it does take time and trouble. A key word here is 'stakeholders'. These are people who have at least the potential to be a strong influence on the organization. In particular they are people who are interested and even challenged or threatened by the results you are trying to achieve. They can see what you are trying to do as being either in their interest or against their interests.

Network power, or being well networked, is emerging as a very important source of power in organizations, especially as the rigid hierarchical model is changing. Sometimes it seems that the process of building up networks is unnecessarily time consuming. Not everyone is likely to be of equal value to you. There may be people who appear to be genuinely positive about what you are trying to do but have themselves little influence. But there may be people with much influence who are opposed to what you are trying to achieve. These are the ones you have to work on.

Physical power can be summarized as 'I have power over you if I am bigger and stronger' but is more prevalent in the army or the prison service, where physical strength is valued and remains embedded in the culture, than in industry, commerce or the public sector. It is sadly true, however, that some forms of physical power are discovered in bullying or sexual harassment in the office. Although distasteful, they are a source of physical power.

The whole purpose of examining the connection between

power and influence in such detail is to think about the basis of the relationship between manager and managed. In a traditional role culture it is difficult to manage upwards. In other cultures it is possible to use different influence strategies to do this. For instance, if the manager recognizes the expert power of a subordinate then he or she will be more likely to respond positively to a proposal made by them and hence the upward process will be helped. This is very important when you think in terms of precisely what you want to achieve.

WHAT DO YOU REALLY DO AS A MANAGER AND WHO LETS YOU DO IT?

It seems from the way organizations are developing, that they have to achieve their results not only through the efforts of people who work for them but also through those who work alongside and above them and even people who are not part of their organization at all. It is not an option to say at the end of an unsuccessful project: 'I failed to achieve this project but it wasn't my fault because those people in that company over there, who I depended upon for this result, wouldn't co-operate.' An example would be within an organization where there is a need to get support and commitment from the very top managers. These people could not be part of your 'command' but if you can't influence them then you have very little chance to be effective.

Already we can begin to paint a picture that shows management is not simply an exercise in giving instruction downwards. It is certainly getting the support and commitment of people who are hierarchically below us but also of those who are hierarchically equal, hierarchically superior and with whom we have no hierarchical connection whatsoever. A simple way of looking at the work of a manager is provided in three powerful questions posed by Rosemary Stewart:

O   What choices do you make?
O   What demands are put upon you?
O   What constraints do you work under?

Pause for a moment and try to answer these questions in your current job.

Choices may be about content – what you do; or about method – how you are going to do it; or about timing – whether to do it now or later; or about contacts – whether to deal with him or her.

Sometimes the demands are explicit:. 'Do that.' Sometimes they are implicit: 'From what she is saying and from the way she is behaving I think she wants me to . . .' And they can be from the boss, colleagues or subordinates.

Constraints may sometimes be challenged: 'Should I do this without telling the boss?', 'Do I have to do it this way?', 'Do I always have to come when you call?'

Giving careful thought to these three questions may make you realize that your job may be broadly defined from above but there are some things that you can do to change it. Maybe you can challenge upwards! Maybe you can start managing upwards?

For many people who see management as a power downward process, the answers to these questions are limited by imagining that they operate in a way that is largely mapped out for them by 'those people up there' who draw the maps. If you see management as a downward process only, then many of the constraints you operate under will be both strong and limiting. If, on the other hand, you see management as a process that moves energy around, downwards, upwards and sideways, then you see that you have more choices and less constraints but probably more demands. So, as you enlarge the scope of the possibilities of management, you widen the range but (usually) you also have to take more responsibility. This is an important aspect and consequence of managing upwards. You have the right to assert certain ideas, values and issues but you also have to share in the responsibility for the outcomes.

TWO VIEWS OF THE WAY ORGANIZATIONS ARE HELD TOGETHER

The role of middle managers in the context of managing upwards has been very well described by Honda's president, Tadashi Kume, in Mintzberg and Quinn's book *The Strategy Process; Concepts, Contexts, Cases*:[1]

> I continually create dreams but people run in different directions unless they
> are able to direct the way they interact with reality. Top management doesn't
> know what bottom management is doing and the opposite is also true. For
> instance, John at Honda, Ohio, is not able to see the company's overall
> direction. We at corporate headquarters see the world differently, think
> differently and face a different environment. It is middle management that is
> charged with integrating the two viewpoints emanating from top and bottom;
> there can be no progress without such integration.
>
> Middle-up-down management is a type of organizational information creation
> that involves the total organization. It may best embody the essence of an
> organization spontaneously surviving in the business environment despite
> change, change and even more change.

This is a very important and not well known definition. The
middle of an organization, its middle management, is where
communication succeeds or fails. The top links to the bottom
through the middle. Without upward management which leads to
upward communication, the corporate organization is dislocated.
Mintzberg himself writes:[2]

> The essential logic of management is that top management creates a visional
> dream and middle management creates and implements concrete concepts to
> solve the dream and transcends the contradictions arising from gaps between
> what exists at the moment and what management hopes to achieve. In other
> words, top management creates an overall theory, while middle management
> creates a mid-range theory and tests it empirically within the framework within
> an entire organization . . . then makes sure that top management knows what is
> really going on.

Both writers suggest that there are different roles for different
types of managers in organizations. Integration of these roles is
vital for the survival of organizations and integration is not the
same process as pushing commands down and leaving it at that.
Later in this book you will find examples of organizations that have
failed to create a culture where managing upwards is a genuine
possibility. It is not a case of somebody wishing to manage
upwards more often or wishing to do it in a more effective way.
The organization has to take some positive steps towards admitting
the value of managing upwards and then act upon it. It also has to
create the necessary culture that will sustain this.

So, if we can shake off the single idea of the role culture – our
bosses must be right because they are our bosses – we can see
great potential for managers and non-managers alike to contribute
to the achievements of the organization. It is not sufficient for you
to realize this, however; you have to persuade others too –
especially your bosses.

REFERENCES

1 Mintzberg, H. and Quinn, J. B. (1991), *The Strategy Process: Concepts, Contexts, Cares,* London: Prentice Hall International.
2 Ibid, p.129.

3

WHAT DO MANAGERS REALLY MANAGE?

❖

If the only answer you can give to this question is 'the people who work for them', then you don't need this book. Give it to someone who does. When I was first involved in management training, there were six 'm's in answer to this question and the first three were men, money and machinery. It seems laughably out of date now.

The starting point to answer the question is people and other resources. Then by exploding the People box you can identify a number of quite different areas where people manage. As we go through a list of 'What managers manage', it might be interesting to check at the same time where the possibilities for upward management most obviously lie.

Managers manage the following:

○   Systems and procedures
○   Peoples' energy
○   Teams
○   Change
○   Time
○   Learning processes
○   Other resources

Some of these may appear more obviously 'downward' than

others but I shall explain how all of them afford opportunities for managing upward.

SYSTEMS AND PROCEDURES

For many, especially supervisory managers, this is what management consists of. It concerns pressing the buttons on the systems and making things happen. (I do not refer here to computer systems in particular but any management system from a simple box office to a complicated Value Added Tax office.) This may be an area where managing upwards is not particularly easy as the system may well be imposed on the manager by a system maker. There may be opportunities or even real needs, however, that may make you want to adapt or modify the system to correspond exactly to your needs today. Systems that once were well designed can drift out of date.

Sometimes starting a new management job is a bit like putting on an old coat. It doesn't quite fit, it's not quite clean and it's not quite stylish but it will do for now and one day (soon) we'll put it right. And somehow we get used to it, often quickly, and we forget that it's not really the way we would like it.

PEOPLES' ENERGY

It is not difficult to walk through a department or part of an organization to assess whether or not it has energy. Some departments fire and explode with energy, some are lost in a soup of sleepiness. The manager is there to release people's energy, to bring the most out of them, to manage their morale. In Japan, much of the work that has gone into thinking about management is based on the premise that in organizations there are some very energetic and strong people who do things with energy and strength outside of work and when they come into work they hang it up on the hook with their coat. How do you release the energy, the strength and the morale of people in the workplace?

TEAMS

Managing teams is an area where management must be upward and downward. Team management may involve setting clear objectives and helping people who are falling behind but it also involves listening to the contribution of team members, and listening to the difficulties of the team member. Sadly, some of the most thrusting and effective systems managers are good at what they do because they are quick and sure and well structured but they don't always listen to the people in their organization. On the other hand, the people who are best equipped to listen often are not the most thrusting and structured. This is a contradiction that has been identified by team management research.

One of the difficulties of a team that is starting to develop well is the way in which it handles conflict and disagreement. Immature teams frequently don't confront things as well as they could because they fear the consequences. This is especially true for junior members of these teams because they simply don't know how to talk directly to the team leader. Opportunities for managing upwards will be limited in immature teams.

CHANGE

Change is another difficult abstraction. There is ample evidence to show that many of the problems associated with change are due to the fact that people on whom change is targeted, are fearful of the processes involved. But they are not sufficiently taken into account and they are not able to express their views, even though they may not visibly resist the change.

One way of looking at the players in the change management process is to think of three types of people:

○ Change sponsors, who initiate change
○ Change agents, who are asked to carry out change
○ Change targets, who will be changed.

In a downward management situation you can see how this could become a simple downward process. It is unlikely, however, that change is as simple as telling people what they have to do. It is much more likely that change agents (which is what most managers are) will have to act in both a downward and upward way. They are part of the overall communication system which is vital in change projects to avoid resistance caused by fear and misunderstanding. There is certainly a role for upward and downward management in the management of change issues.

TIME

There are three ways of thinking about time management in organizations (see Figure 3.1), two of which are important in managing upwards. The first way is called 'me'. It covers actions that you do on your own and no one but you is going to prevent you from getting them right, for example, having a place to put things, having some sort of programme for the day, having a system for effectively handling paper, not putting matters off and not avoiding difficult issues.

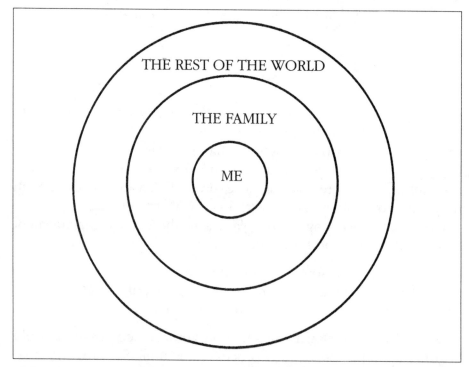

Figure 3.1   People you have to influence

The second way concerns relationships in the workplace and effective time management. We call this 'the family'. This family is the group of people with whom you work on a daily basis. Thus, if you work in the Birmingham branch of an organization and your boss is in London, your boss is not part of the family. The family lets me do deals on working effectively. I can ask them to leave me in peace for an hour while I finish a task properly and I will do the same for them.

Similarly, boss relationships are tested by the family. Take the following situation. In the course of a morning I, who am Mary's boss, discover something in my work that she would benefit from knowing. So I tell her, which interrupts her work. Fifteen minutes later I discover something else which is of interest to Mary and I tell her that too. At the end of the morning I have interrupted her fourteen times. It would have been far better to realize what was going on and say to her: 'Mary, there are matters arising that you need to know about. Let's meet for half an hour at three o'clock and I'll show them to you all in one go.'

The third way, and most important in an upward management context, is called 'the rest of the world' and the rest of the world are the people over whom you have least control. Your boss says to you: 'I need a report of that incident for a meeting before anything else tomorrow', and you know from a professional point of view that the report cannot be done in that time. You could give your boss a summary or extract of the report but the report itself would take at least two days. If you agree to the request you are lying, you are not helping the managing upward process and you are contributing to wrecking organizational understanding and value. If you say to your boss: 'I do not think that what you are asking can be done in one day. I could give you a useful summary, if you like, and finish it off the following day', you are managing upwards in a professional way.

I once asked a group of very senior managers if, when their boss said 'Come now' they could ever say 'Can I just finish this off?' or 'Could I come in five minutes when I've made a telephone call?'. They all replied that when the boss said 'Come now' he meant now, until one of them admitted that they had never actually said 'Could I come in five minutes?'.

Power is not evenly distributed – this is a recurring theme. If you don't try to manage upwards by saying 'Could I just finish this?', you maintain the power-management downward process and your boss is not given the information necessary to make a decision. They assume that because you decided to come, you were available. Managing upwards verifies that this is the best way for both of you to perform.

LEARNING PROCESSES

These could be the managers' own learning processes or the learning processes of people who work for them. We sometimes call this coaching. It would be hard to conceive of a genuine coaching or learning relationship where the whole process is downward. You have to take account of the abilities of learners, the perception of learners, the constraints that learners can put upon themselves and, although coaching may require an overall sense of direction which may be offered in a downward manner, it is beyond doubt that coaching is also an upward managing occurrence.

OTHER ITEMS

There are certainly other items that managers manage, for instance, information has become a serious issue with developments in information technology. They manage quality, they manage influencing interactions with other people and it becomes obvious as this list develops, that merely managing downwards is an insufficient process to draw in the full range of energies and abilities that the organization can offer.

FINDING OUT

In this book we shall look at many organizations and how they have succeeded or failed in managing upwards and at some of the skills that are required to succeed. It is an irony that most managers are both managers and managed and are thus involved in a process managing upwards, downwards and sideways.

Working with a UK government agency, I had the opportunity to listen to its director-general addressing his managers on a number of occasions. On one particular occasion, he admitted how much he had learned from 'people who work for me'. Now this may be because he had taken the responsibility, somehow, for learning – explicitly or implicitly – from his staff but there is also an issue there where you can see things moving upwards. During the period of my involvement with the agency there was a conversation between a very senior manager and the director-general that went something like this:

SENIOR MANAGER: Is it really true that quite recently such and such an event happened?

DIRECTOR-GENERAL: It is true.

SENIOR MANAGER: It is appalling in my view that senior management was not informed that this was going to happen.

DIRECTOR-GENERAL: I am very surprised if this has been the case. Certainly you should have been told, you are quite right. However, had you no idea at all that this sort of event was about to take place?

SENIOR MANAGER: Yes, I have heard a rumour, or half information.

DIRECTOR-GENERAL: Then, why didn't you ask?

It is often unreasonable to expect senior or top management to be paragons, remembering to tell everyone everything. Sometimes they forget and sometimes they are just too busy but if the organization has a rumour or an expectation circulating, then the upward management process says 'let's go and find out about it'.

A very simple example of a failure to manage upwards was presented to me by a regional director of a state-owned bank in West Africa. He explained that the bank's managing director had recently been to his region and had visited one or two of the larger branches. The managing director then returned to the capital without seeing or talking to any of the branch staff. This was offered as an example of distant, uncaring, head-office type management. Nobody had said to the managing director, while he was in one of these branches, that the branch staff would like to meet him. The branch manager had made no attempt to ask him if he would like to meet the staff. When I asked the managing director about this, he said that he would have been delighted to.

This is an example of an artificial constraint being applied to a branch manager, which he should at least have tried to challenge. It is not even likely that all challenges will be appropriately achieved but one of the responsibilities at this level is to ask upwards: 'Could you spend half an hour talking to the staff?'

A large organization had a new chief executive and his style was quite different from that of any other chief executive they had known. He was certainly less driven by the traditional rules of internal bureaucracy. Although even after a short time he was achieving significant results for the organization, there was some misunderstanding and unease about some aspects of his management style. In a meeting with senior managers he asked for some information and figures on a particular subject. Six weeks later he realized that the information had not been given to him. When he asked why he was told nothing had been done because the request hadn't been confirmed in writing.

This is another sad example of a failure to manage upwards. There was nothing to stop the senior managers checking after the meeting to find out exactly what he wanted. They could have asked him to confirm in writing his exact request so that there could be no misunderstanding. They could even have added 'and you will receive the data two weeks from today'. And they were not supervisors or junior managers.

In my work I hear of many examples of managers who have made life difficult for subordinate managers and I wonder whether these actions are generated by malice or simply from carelessness. While malice is not unknown in organizational relationships, it does seem that many problems arise out of management carelessness. The carelessness is compounded because of an absence of a managing upwards component and the problems of carelessness are, therefore, almost inevitably worsened.

DUMPING IT UPWARDS

Another example comes from a dynamic and exciting software and information technology development company. Created by its proprietor, it was for a long time a one person, one product firm. The one product has sold well and the company has opened up new markets and after-sales services and is currently going through a heart-searching approach to the challenges of developing a new product range to replace and compete with the existing ones.

There is no value in drawing an organizational chart of this company. Suffice to say that it runs into management crises every six months and each time they say: 'We really should sort out our problem of communication, or teamwork, or planning, or whatever it might be.' At the end of the day, all the problems in this company are pushed upwards on to the shoulders of the managing director. This is a bad example of managing upwards and is called 'Scapegoating'; they blame him for everything. Although it is as part of a managing upwards process that we see these negative aspects of managing upwards – scapegoating and blaming – it is sad that we do not see enough of the positive examples that managing upwards offers.

Since I started thinking about managing upwards, the One Minute Manager series has been extended with an important small volume by K. Blanchard, W. Oncken and H. Burrows, entitled *The One Minute Manager Meets the Monkey*. The monkey or, more accurately, the set of monkeys that sit on the shoulders of the senior manager, are the problems that he or she has taken over from members of staff; to the extent that they go off and play golf on Saturday while he has to go to work. The purpose of *The One Minute Manager Meets the Monkey* is to work out whose monkeys are whose and what to do about them. This is another example of managers pulling work upwards when they are actually being used by subordinate managers in the organization as a way of ducking their own particular responsibilities.

It is all very well saying what managing upwards could or should entail but there are a number of problems that must be solved before organizations will see its value and advantages. It is no use shouting at your manager in frustration that you could have been told about this much earlier, in language that will anger him. We need to know how to confront openly and fairly and how to assert the rights that we have, the rights that middle managers have to do a good job properly. So why isn't managing upwards a more usual process in business? Why are we waiting for our boss or the organization to tell us what to do? The answer is bound up with organizational design and organizational culture.

DRAWING ORGANIZATIONAL CHARTS

It is quite interesting to ask people how long have organization charts – in the way that we draw them now, with boxes and lines – been used. Boxes and lines are the very processes that reinforce the management downwards culture. Although there have been organizations for thousands of years you do not find examples of our modern organization charts. The Egyptians were obviously organized enough to build the pyramids but despite the fact that they had organizations, they didn't draw them on charts as we do now.

There is not much evidence of boxes and lines and organization charts before the mid-1930s, in the United States. This is when organizations were being put together with much respect for the Industrial Engineering school of thought developed by F. W. Taylor. The whole purpose of Taylor's work was to de-skill people's jobs as much as possible – leaving the bottom-line workers to do just that – the work. You have to remember that the bottom line of the organization charts at that time, the people who actually did the work, were largely immigrants to the US with problems of quality of craft standards and certainly with problems of language. So it seemed perfectly reasonable in the 1930s to put in middle management layers and to de-skill the thinking process from the people doing the operations. Thus the middle management way was born and by its very existence created downward management.

It now seems that middle management, in order to feather its nest and build its empire, has become part of the managing down process and is not well designed to reciprocate the managing up process. In Chapter 4 we look at a number of organizations that have tried, consciously, to remove constraints from the middle layer in order to promote and encourage the managing upwards process.

DIFFERING LEVELS OF MANAGERS IN ORGANIZATIONS

It is easy to presume that management is management and that you can change organization, or change level within an organization, and the process of management simply copies itself. This is true to a certain extent. If you use Rosemary Stewart's questions (p.11) about demands, choices and constraints, we suppose it is true to the extent that every manager we meet would be able to answer them. Different types of industry and types of work, however, demand different styles and approaches to management and some of these may be more supportive of upward management than others. Supervising in a primary industry such as coal mining, for instance, may present different opportunities for managing upwards from, say, working on a newspaper. Probably there are different stresses and tensions which, according to the situation, may call for upward or not-upward management.

There are, without doubt, certain differences between the work managers do and their level of seniority within the hierarchy or organization, and this has certain implications for managing upwards. If we take first very senior managers or directors, their role is implied in the word 'director'. They are there to give the business or organization a sense of direction. This is not always easy. In very calm business conditions, which are probably unlikely to occur again in the future, you can imagine directors of organizations setting their directions from time to time, making adjustments and basically ploughing the same furrow. In more turbulent times the seeking of direction is fraught with difficulty and it is not unusual for directors to imagine a course of action to be possible, or advantageous, only to have to regress and move to another course of action. This is not desirable. Strategic management should be more long term in the way it operates – but that is not always possible.

If you then move to middle management (and I shall come back to a gap between directors and middle management, who we shall call senior middle management, in a moment), they are there to set objectives for supervisory management to put into action. They are not necessarily managing the work of hands-on workers. Their work is to set objectives, set up control systems and timetables, to delegate, to monitor, to appraise, to allocate resources and so on.

Supervisory management's rule is to 'get the work done'. It entails motivating people; encouraging, praising, occasionally kicking, pushing and criticizing. This level of management ensures work is completed on time, is of good quality etc.

So, within the organization there are distinctly different types of management operation. One is called setting directions, which may be long term (three to five years) and vague, another is setting objectives which are precise and often short term (six to twelve months), and the other is ensuring action in the workplace.

An important level of management not so far included in this description is the senior middle management. I have already said that directors, or senior managers, often create turbulence and that middle managers set objectives. The role of senior middle managers is to tidy up some of the turbulence and provide stability for middle managers, by giving them a sense of priority and a sense of where to apply their efforts. They provide an important filter between top and middle management, preventing the middle managers from being rushed back and forth by the turbulence that influences directors.

One of the problems with this level of management is that it often does not see this particularly important turbulence-eliminating role and sees itself either as part of top management or as part of middle management. They often see themselves as part of top management, because they like to feel part of the top level, or as part of middle management, because they feel particularly competent in this arena.

All of this suggests a proper place for upward as well as downward management. Tadeshi Kumi says that top management sets direction, supervisory management actions the work and middle and senior middle management are the honeycomb of the organization, transmitting energy and ideas upwards and downwards. Communications are more often the responsibility of middle and senior middle managers than top managers or bottom managers. They are the communication system that joins the top and the bottom.

So, managing upwards is a beneficial movement for organizations. It sets out to say that the power of management within an organization is enhanced if it is seen not only as a downward process but also a return process and a sideways process. In the following chapters we look at the way organizations have structured themselves to enable the process of upward management to take place; we show some of the mechanisms that seem necessary to make this happen; and look at some of the skills involved in managing upwards. Finally, we shall look at ways of bringing about the organizational change that will allow managing upwards to be recognized.

4

UP AND DOWN THE
ORGANIZATION

❖

It is, unfortunately, not sufficient to realize that there is great potential in managing upwards or simply to realize that management is not merely a power downwards issue. You have also to understand some of the skills of managing upwards and you have to know how and when to take responsibility for asserting and getting your message upwards. You have to be able to communicate well. The organization has to support this style of management.

There are organizations and organizational cultures that are supportive of the idea of managing upwards. There are certain organizations, however, where it is practically impossible to manage upwards because of the accidental design of the organization and others where it is impossible to manage upwards because of the deliberate design of the organization. A bizarre and extreme example of this would be Hitler's Germany. Trying to manage upwards would have been folly. In this chapter we look at some types of organizations that have tried particularly hard to encourage reverse communication processes and thereby endorse the idea of managing upwards.

GIVING MANAGERS PERMISSION TO MANAGE UPWARDS

Jonathan Coates and Associates (JCA) worked recently on a management development programme with a large construction company. The design of the programme was fairly conventional. We met with a group of about fifteen senior managers every two months, for two or three days at a time, in an isolated training centre. The programme consisted of modules on communication, finance, marketing, strategy and so on.

Quite early in the programme, the managing director chose to spend some of the evenings of the sessions in a semi-social, semi-professional manner with these senior managers. (We should say here that the managers did not report directly to the managing director but to the layer below him.) The managing director was a very conscientious and hard-working man; he certainly worked harder than anybody else in the company.

During dinner one evening, one of the engineers present described a problem to do with the costing of structure of projects which in her view was a poor use of a design system – wasteful of time and effort – which should be put right. The managing director listened carefully and with concern to this perfectly fair description of a system that wasn't working well. Finally he said: 'I know, I know, it's worrying me too. It's just that we are trying to do so many other matters at the moment.'

You could sense the frustration of both parties; one wanting to change the way the work was done and the other wanting to do it but not having the time. We asked the engineer whether she would be able to do something, if asked, to help solve the system problem. She thought she could. In fact she had already put a considerable amount of thinking into it. It would be a question of giving her the go-ahead to solve this kind of problem. We asked the managing director: 'Why don't you ask her to do it?' He looked very nervous and said: 'How would I know what she was doing? How would I know that this important issue is being solved properly by someone who has never done it before?'

We asked her if she could write out a simple two-page proposal for the project, outlining the eventual outcome, the steps involved, the amount of time it would take her and identifying the other resources she would want to use. She said that this would not be a problem and was very pleased at being asked to do it. He was still uncertain.

One week later he had her proposal for changing the costing structure. It would take three months; she would use her current project as a model; it would take one week of her time in total and would therefore delay the completion of her current project by one week. Also it would require input from the finance group and some help from the systems team, both of which were understanding and supportive of her ideas. She then proposed that she spend an additional one month after the completion of this specific project, to incorporate the changes and produce a general version of the costing system. Her estimate was that the whole change would cost in the order of £10,000 but would reduce the overhead on similar projects by about 10 per cent.

Much more confidently, the managing director gave his approval and added a suggestion of his own. He monitored the adaptations to the particular project and called a special meeting of all senior engineers before embarking on the second phase, which was to incorporate these ideas generally.

This kind of permission-giving process, where managers are free to identify problems but then to offer them upward as solutions and not as problems, is a very important issue in managing upwards. I am not proposing anarchy: that would be a very dangerous way for organizations to behave. In this case, using first a formal proposal and second a series of checkpoints and milestones, the project can be carefully controlled. Sometimes it is hard to distinguish between upwards and downwards in this sort of process. The request was coming upwards, the permission was being offered downwards and the work was being pushed upwards.

The real problem is that managers grow to expect what their role should be. They learn that this is what I do, this is what the boss does and they also learn to wait to be told. They get frustrated by the waiting when often they could be offering worked-through solutions.

Such a situation is not helped by the fact that far too many senior managers jump in much too quickly to solve their subordinates' problems for them. They do this either because they can do it, or because they think it is their job to help subordinates solve their problems. Either way, this process seals the levels and floors between up and down managers. It does nothing for management development either!

As this same construction company developed as an organization, more and more problems identified by managers as becoming problems to their work were offered upwards to senior management, not as problems but as solutions or a set of options for solutions. In this way, the organization began to listen to the ideas of its middle management and began to expect them to come up with solutions not problems.

A final example from this exercise with the construction company involved marketing. At the time of the JCA programme, they were short of business and nervous about it. We realized that the people in the organization who were nearest to particular specialized markets were the engineers and architects themselves. So we taught them some basic marketing skills and concepts and helped them to draw up individual marketing plans. They enjoyed doing their own marketing, instead of leaving it to people who they did not always know well and who they also felt didn't know their customers very well. They were surprised to discover that marketing wasn't so very mysterious and were pleased to use some more of their own potential in the development of the company.

After the above examples it is hardly surprising that listening in a positive way is a feature of the process of managing upwards. (Chapter 8 includes listening as an interactive skill between people in the workplace.)

Many organizations have sealed themselves into a management downward culture probably by accident. Strong role cultures where 'the boss is the boss' are good at this, so it is evident that in these cultures managers are going to have to work hard or cleverly to manage upwards.

HOW NOT TO LISTEN IN YOUR ORGANIZATION

Our first example is of a large and hierarchically designed organization such as a bank, building society or any other large, regionally spread out organization (see Figure 4.1). We find in this (slightly stylized) arrangement that the head of the organization, the chief general manager, resides at the top of the head-office skyscraper. Below him (and they *are* usually male), there are general managers, then group managing directors, then senior managers, junior managers, messengers and supervisors. It seems that the top management have to be at the top of the skyscraper, partly to be near God and partly to be as far away from their customers as they can get.

As this type of organization spreads out into the country, we have first a regional operation and then within this a series of district operations. Next, we have the individual branches of which there may be two thousand. Ultimately, in the branch, on the front desk, talking to customers are the junior staff – by now a very long way from the top management. Finally, there come the customers themselves.

Despite the fact that these organizations are large, their bureaucratic, downward and outward communications systems are very powerful and very rapid. The chief general manager has an idea. He consults and decides. Plans are made and instructions are pushed out from head office, through the regional structure,

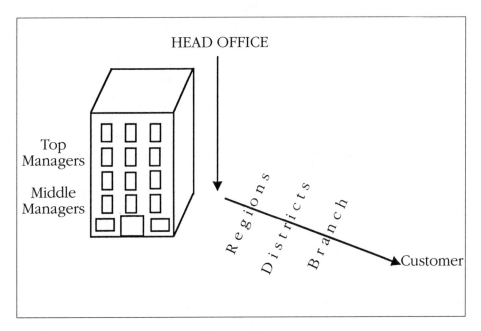

Figure 4.1   Downward and outward communication in an organization

through the district structure, into the branch structure and they become an instruction to a member of staff. Perhaps it results in a communication being posted on a counter for customers to see, or perhaps it is given out or explained by the branch manager.

Messages, instructions and commands reach the far corners of the organization very quickly. Regrettably, the reverse communication position is not quite the same. The customer talking to the cashier says: 'Why don't you in your bank have such and such a service? They have one at Bank *X*, down the road'. And the cashier, who likes talking to customers because they, after all, provide the basis for the business, says: 'That's a good idea, I don't know why we don't have such a service, I shall make a suggestion and pass on your idea. Thank you'. And the suggestion is duly made to the branch manager, or the deputy branch manager, and you can just see the idea going back up to the district, back up to the region, back up to the head office and back up to the chief general manager.

You can't see it happening? You don't believe it happens? You're right. Somewhere between the keen cashier and the branch manager and the district manager, the idea fizzles out. Why? It is a perfectly fair and reasonable idea; it is an idea that has come directly from what the market is talking about. One of the reasons that it fizzles out is that the communication system only works one way; it is only designed to tell people what to do and not to listen.

Branch managers are busy running the business of banking. The ideas are half formulated. They don't have any system structure or design. They are only a rough and ready idea. You can't just plug them in. They would have to be discussed, designed properly and approved. They would have to be assessed against the business plan and the corporate plan. It seems that the system is designed to prevent them happening. Sometimes upward ideas appear to be an infernal nuisance.

Although this illustration describes problems with upward communication in large, bureaucratic organizations, there is also a general lesson. This is that many of the ideas unsuccessfully pushed upwards in organizations of all sizes, are not ready for implementation and the organization has not set up any processes to make them ready for an implementation decision. You can see the organization and the way that it transmits messages, with a system of doors that only open in one direction, like non-return valves or even computer systems being designed to flow in one direction only. It is hardly surprising that these types of organizations don't listen very carefully inside themselves and therefore any issue called managing upwards or proposing solutions to problems, is unlikely to be a great success. If this is a stereotype of an organization at work, we will now look at some actual organizations where they have tried very hard to design an organizational shape or structure, where active listening and therefore management upwards, is an integral part of the issue.

ORGANIZATIONS WHICH HAVE DESIGNED THEMSELVES TO LISTEN TO UPWARD MESSAGES

THE CAR HIRE COMPANY

This is a well-known, international car hire company which encourages all its managers to spend one week, twice a year, doing the jobs of the managers who report to them. Thus, the regional director in a regional centre would spend one week, twice a year, actually sitting at a desk in a bright coloured jacket, issuing cars, checking cars in from service and cleaning, and taking them to auction. This company calls the process 'listening'. It doesn't do it very often and it doesn't ask managers to do the jobs of many layers down, just the layer reporting directly to them.

THE COMPUTER COMPANY

This computer manufacturer, based in the eastern United States, has a classic organization chart. There is a president and four vice-presidents and the company is divided into many product divisions. It employs one thousand people, of which three or four hundred are research scientists or engineers. Most of the scientists are the brightest people that you can recruit, Ph.D. and double Ph.D. The dress code is jeans and T-shirts and the work environment encourages people to work when they feel like it – three or four days at a stretch, drop out, come back when you're ready.

The problem with this type of company is keeping aware, up to the minute or up to the second, about what is going on. The president spends most of his time looking at the world in which computers are being developed, looking around at what customers are doing, what uses there are and what competitors are producing but he also needs to know his own capability and what his own company can produce. So twice a year, for two months, he takes off his business suit, puts on his jeans and T-shirt, delegates his presidential role to his four vice presidents and works at what appears to be the bottom of the organization. It is important to know that the president had been a graduate research scientist and had worked his way through the ranks of the organization, otherwise he could spend no useful time at the bottom of the organization.

This is not the boss visiting his troops to have tea and biscuits to find out what is happening. Sometimes he leads a research team, sometimes he works alone, sometimes he works in someone else's research team. When people ask him: 'Why do you spend so much time at the bottom of your organization?', he says, 'I don't. For four months of the year I make it the top of the organization. I need to find out what we are really good at, what we are capable of, what we could develop. And I can't do it if I have to rely on reports and subcommittees'.

If these ideas appeal to you don't rush out and start copying car hire or computer research companies. Work out for yourself where there are possibilities for encouraging, in a structured way, the flow of upward driven ideas and solutions to your particular problems.

THE RETAILER

Another organization is a large retailer which effectively has two boards of management. One is in fact called the Management Committee – this runs the organization and consists of all the heads of departments that operate the company – but they are not the Board. The managing director chairs both the Management Committee and the Board so that both teams are kept informed.

If the Management Committee spend most of their time running the business, what does the Board do? Well, the seven members of the Board spend most of the time in the high street, finding out what the customer is doing. They look at customers; they watch what they do in stores and what they do and don't buy. They talk to shop assistants about what sells well or badly, on the basis that people selling goods in Leeds know more about people buying garments in Leeds than anyone else in the organization. The fact that this particular brand sells poorly in Leeds, whereas last week it was selling well in Edinburgh, really makes very little difference to the person selling it in Leeds.

This company has a very effective reporting system and reports on product sales come-back quickly, first to the Management Committee and then to the Board. Why then do the Board spend so much time in their own – and also their competitors' – stores? The reason is that they want to see it as it happens. They want to see what is happening right now, in the here and now, and not when it arrives later as a report on something which has already happened. This is another example of an organization trying to get validity into its information upwards processes and in this case they do it by what is more or less a bypass, a direct line to the top of the organization because the top of the organization comes down to see what is going on.

These are some examples of organizations where people are encouraged to listen in to the organization and find out what is going on. These activities are not the result of chance or good luck, they are designed into the structure.

LISTENING FOR GOOD IDEAS

A final example of this kind of process comes from a British company that places emphasis on encouraging ideas coming through the company and also thinks carefully about the change implications that stem from these ideas. Four times a year the staff of this company are asked the same question: In your part of the organization what represents a strength that we are not exploiting, or a weakness we are not taking enough notice of? It is a local 'strength and weakness' analysis and it is important to realize that staff are only allowed to reply from their own part of the organization and may not make comments on other parts of the organization.

They get a surprisingly, and consistently, high response, often finding returns of about 20 per cent of people asked. There is no money for anyone involved in this programme. If you think that 20 per cent is a low figure, experience with these types of projects says that you might get a higher figure the first time you do it, somewhat less the second time, and it peters out on the third. So to achieve consistent figures of around 20 per cent is very interesting indeed.

The problem now is what to do with this half-formed data and one of the reasons why organizations don't push ideas upwards is that they are in such poor shape. When they push ideas downwards, they have carefully prepared them through committees, working parties and system designers, and whatever the product requires. So in this particular company a small working party of line managers is seconded totally to looking at this data and – this is regarded as an organizational blessing – if you get on to one of these working parties you are seen to be doing well.

Thus the organization gives this upward ideas process some time and the team sorts the raw data into categories: store or branch design; cash handling; reactions to ideas from customers; opportunities or possibilities that are not being tackled, and so on. There is no agreement that they must choose the largest pile but they can choose only one pile and the other contributors are sent polite letters saying: 'Thank you for your ideas. This time we are not looking at these. We are going to look at this one'. They then invite those who contributed ideas on the chosen problem to work on regional working parties to attempt to take their ideas forward and to make some sense of them. Thus you might find that there is a Scottish working group, there may be two or three in the North of England, and so on. The working groups are given resources if they ask for them: an accountant, architect, computer systems person, or a market researcher for instance, could be made available.

As the projects begin to develop, the regional teams start to group themselves at pooling their ideas until there is finally just one working group, working on a very sophisticated product and organizational design. It is possible for the product ideas not to reach this stage if they turn out to be unfeasible. Assuming that they do get to this stage, however, the ideas are now in a highly developed form, with costings, budgets and scenarios and they are taken, if appropriate, to the company Board for approval.

The Board has not agreed to agree to these ideas just because they are being presented to them as a result of this process. They have to compete with other ideas coming to the Board for resources. The experience has been that most of them do get favourable consideration, however, and many of them are approved by the Board but this is not the end of the process.

The various people who have so far worked on developing the idea return to their normal jobs while the project is being turned into reality and this may take months or even years. The outcome is that at a later a date a whole team of strangers comes into a store or branch or depot and it is at this stage that the people who have worked on the initial committees say to their friends and colleagues: 'Hey, come and look at this. You remember when I was working on that idea? Well here it is, beginning to happen'. So, not only does the company derive many of its change ideas from within, it has also implanted a whole army of change agents who are able to take ownership of the project, rather than to say: 'What are they up to now?' or 'My goodness, what have they thought of this time?'.

There is a certain consistency behind all these examples, where the organization is prepared to put in time and effort to reverse some of the telling types of one-way, or monolithic, organization design processes that we have become used to.

EXAMPLES FROM JAPAN

You only have to read the simplest textbooks on some of the advances in Japanese management to see that this sort of process is encouraged in Japanese organizations too. If you draw a 'typical' manufacturing organization in an hierarchic pyramid or triangle (see Figure 4.2) you find three types of managers:

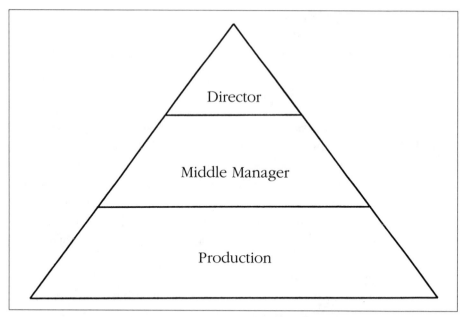

Figure 4.2   Conventional organizational layering

O   Directors who provide an overall strategy
O   Middle managers who provide various services such as R &
       D, training, accounting
O   Production managers who supervise the manufacturing
       workers and processes.

The problem with this structure is that the middle manager layer
separates the top from the bottom. In addition, the middle
manager levels often think that they are part of the authority
structure and enjoy this role. In the example that we are
considering, the company was reorganized to look like the
structure in Figure 4.3.

This puts production and services at an equivalent hierarchical
level but the communication routes have changed. Now, if
production managers require something they make their case to
the service managers. The service group contains the company
bank and money is raised in the 'normal' way. The process returns
esteem to the managers and employees who produce the product.
This company pushes hard for quality in manufacturing and
rewards quality. Not surprisingly, new ideas from the 'bottom'
have a high survival rate in this organization.

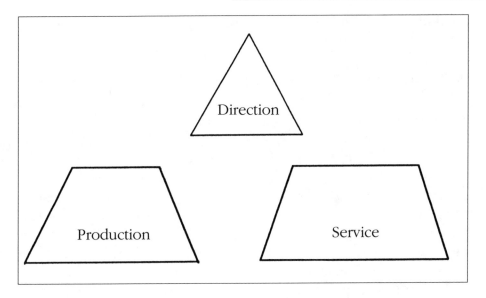

Figure 4.3   Making middle management service the producer

In five years, the Toyota Corporation through various initiatives had 20,000 ideas come upward from its employees. They implemented or sanctioned 70 per cent of these. Some were trivial and the added value was slight. Others made very significant contributions.

SUMMARY

My purpose in this chapter has been to show that most organizations constructed (accidentally or deliberately) in 'normal' hierarchic ways do not easily encourage upwards management. The structures themselves are designed for management and communication to succeed in one direction only. This not only stifles ideas coming upwards within the organization, in service industries it prevents ideas coming up from the customer.

Some companies – but not many – have thought carefully about this and have been able to replace the one way route. I was recently asked by a banking client to name a bank that had thought this through. I had to admit I could not. It is obviously going to be more difficult in traditional, formal, role cultures to break down a traditional way of operating. It is not impossible.

PASSING MESSAGES UPWARDS IN ORGANIZATIONS

There is another matter to do with managing and communicating upwards that many managers find difficult to cope with. This is the problem of trying to explain something which is a cause of concern to senior management. Sometimes the opportunity is planned and managers know that they are going to have a chance to make a case to senior management and sometimes the opportunity is unplanned and the meeting appears to happen in a random way. There are two ways in which managers seem to make a mess of the situation. First of all they go too far with their complaint, are generally aggressive and harass the senior management concerned. Or, faced with the opportunity they bungle completely the chance to make their point.

A couple of examples from our own work at JCA illustrate this well. One occurred during a meeting of a group of managers, largely women, who manage residential homes for a local authority in London. They were given the chance to work together for three days and in that time a number of common concerns became obvious. On the final day they were given the opportunity to present these problems to their own senior management and were quite unable to put their points together in any coherent way.

The other interesting example was a group of senior civil servants at the end of a particularly stimulating training programme where many items relating to change were on the agenda. In the meeting they had no difficulty in generating aggressive energy and emotion concerning several important arenas. At the end of the session, the head of the department, the Under Secretary, came to listen. They had almost nothing to say. It does not sound particularly impressive to management when they realize that time has been given to explore opportunities and problems and nothing comes from it. The silence is as inadequate as the aggression would have been embarrassing.

We have thought about this and have decided upon a step-by-step approach to presenting problems upwards. First of all we encourage managers not to try to solve all the problems of the universe at once. Change is usually the sum of small change-steps, successfully and peacefully achieved.

The first step is to identify a problem that you need to solve. The emphasis is important here; it is not a problem that somebody else might need, or that you have a passing, academic interest in. You must feel that the failure to solve this problem is blocking your work and removing the block will make you more effective. So you must pick a problem which is yours; yours as an individual or yours in the sense of the group of people you normally work with, or a problem between you and your boss. We find that it helps to give a general description of the problem and a recent example. This allows the abstraction of a general problem to be pinned down in a much more concrete way.

The next step is very important and is one of the most frequently omitted. It is to identify the solution that you have in mind. The essence of managing upwards successfully is not to pose problems to one's boss but to identify genuine problems and pose reasonable solutions. Be as specific as possible. The three change 'words' are; more of (and less of), better, and different. Merely stating that there is a problem is just complaining. Stating that there is a problem and offering a solution, or solutions, is managing upwards.

In making the suggestion for this solution, consider your rights, and the rights of other people including those of your boss. For instance, you may say: 'This poor accounting system is preventing me from getting my job done properly.' The point about rights is important and relates to the general subject of assertiveness. If you feel that your rights are the only ones that are important and no one else's are worth taking into account, then you're likely to be aggressive. Equally, if you deny the value of your rights and assume everyone else's to be important, or paramount, then you are likely to be submissive.

When you present the solution to your boss, talk in terms of benefits and not features. Features describe the way the solution would be implemented. Benefits are the results of implementing the solution. So for example, you could say: 'We could move to the office at the other end of the corridor which has a properly designed computer terminal plug', and this fails to take account of

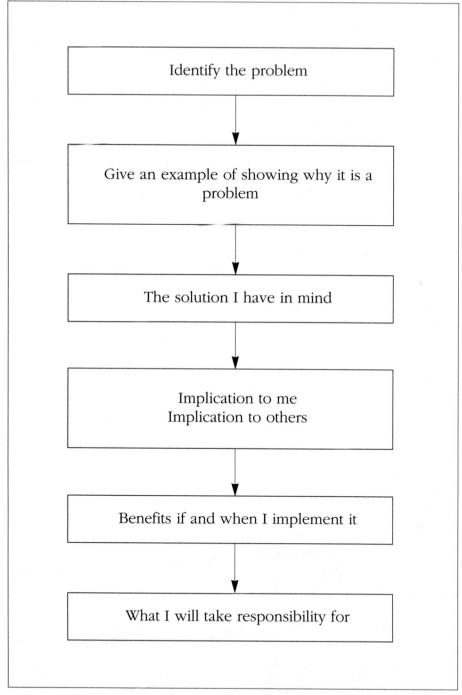

Figure 4.4 The step-by-step approach to passing problems upwards

the benefits of the move. The benefits might be: 'We can obtain easy 24-hour access to the computer, which means that the noise of the printer doesn't distract other people, which in turn means that we can provide a faster, more effective customer service than before.'

In moving to this solution some responsibility inevitably falls on you as the middle manager. What will you take responsibility for in the outcome? What does it commit you to? Should you mention this in the way that you present the problem upwards? You might, for instance, want to say: 'And in what we suggest, we will be responsible for meeting the figures at the end of every evening shift if ...' and then it becomes the basis for a negotiation. To say: 'We want you to help us to solve our problem, boss', is inadequate. Merely to say 'There is a problem', is even more so. We have found that it also adds real weight to your argument or strategy if you can say that you have been able to try it out and it works. 'We have tested this in our Northern office and everyone found that it speeded up the process by 20 per cent.' The scheme or flowchart in Figure 4.4 summarizes and structures the steps I have just explained for making an argument upwards. It could be the basis of an argument or a written report. Think of the detail of the presentation. Should it be one person who presents it? Should it be presented in writing beforehand? This approach to passing problems upwards, which has been tried now by a number of organizations, needs a strong reinforcement of the idea of managing upwards as well as the general improvement of effectiveness in relationships.

5

APPRAISAL AND MANAGING UPWARDS

❖

There is no doubt that the culture of an organization influences the design, usage and credibility of its appraisal systems. Changing the appraisal system, on the other hand, could influence certain types of culture and enable upward management. Appraisal, therefore, could become an instrument of change if organizations, or individuals, want to move toward a more upward management way of working. This chapter focuses on matters relating to appraisal and what it sets out to do, how it does it and what it achieves.

I could have looked at other organizational institutions as well as appraisal – command meetings, team briefing or organization charts and structures – but appraisal is the one area that will create the most opportunities for managing upwards. In many companies, however, appraisal is all in code; it doesn't appear to relate to the world of real managers. It consumes hours of time and acres of paper in pursuing the ritual and it generally does not discuss the undiscussable – the real questions of organizations.

There is now a healthy move away from appraisal, with its implied bureaucracy, to performance management systems where the emphasis is on collaboration and effectiveness. (An example of a performance management system adopted by a US retailer is given at the end of this chapter.)

For the sake of completeness, it is necessary briefly to readdress some of the basic principles of performance appraisal in organizations. For a detailed description you should read *Practical Management Development*, by Jonathan Coates and Kate Houchin, where the subject of appraisal in organizations is fully treated. The starting point is the realization that the process known as performance appraisal can have many purposes.

PURPOSES

Few people give sufficient thought to the purpose behind appraisal schemes. Or, more precisely, purposes, because there are many and while it is not essential that an appraisal scheme attempts to achieve a single purpose, it cannot achieve all the possible purposes without causing confusion. It is surprising to realize that most people could not consistently answer the question: 'What is the purpose behind your organization's appraisal scheme?' They do it mechanically year after year and they never know fully why it is carried out.

Some of the possible purposes that you could design your appraisal scheme to achieve are:

- ◯   a basis for giving people a reward (or punishment)
- ◯   learning and training objectives
- ◯   monitoring and checking on career development
- ◯   improved communication between boss and subordinate
- ◯   allocating specific time for serious consideration of the question 'where are we going and what is happening?'
- ◯   identifying potential
- ◯   looking at people's strengths and weaknesses
- ◯   seeing how well people are managed.

To achieve all of these with a single appraisal scheme is very unlikely. I try to encourage organizations to include the particular objectives of their scheme on the front page of the appraisal documentation.

Appraisal schemes are a way of pulling people through organizations in a useful way. They could be used to test how far people are progressing on a scale called 'That is where we were and this is where we want to be and let's try to make sure that everyone is coming with us'. These schemes could be allowed to formalize a managing upward process. For instance, appraisal is not often associated with generating options for change but there is no reason why this formal management meeting could not generate such options.

Notice that it would not only be difficult to achieve all the above objectives because there are so many but also because some actually conflict. The most obvious example is that between salary decision making and frank, open communication. 'I think that you could use this meeting, Jonathan, to tell me what we need to know. Please be honest. Please be frank. Please tell me how well I have been able to help you as a boss this year and, at the end of this frank discussion, I shall give what I think is the right pay rise, or perhaps I shall make a decision to impose some sort of punishment. However, don't let that worry you, please be as free and frank as you like in the first part of the meeting.'

METHODS OF APPRAISAL

It can be seen that the method of appraisal may be fairly formal and mechanistic. On the other hand, it may be informal using as its recording system a blank piece of paper. The main advantage of appraisal is that it gives people a chance to clear the air, work out what is expected of them, how well they have been doing and where they go next. There is an argument here which goes: we do this anyway and we do it all the time. In a sense this is true but more often it's done all the time against a background of trying to push things out of the door and achieve business targets. There is no doubt at all that in the way that different layers of management perceive what is going on, bosses will frequently say, 'We do this kind of informal appraisal all the time', and subordinates will say, 'We don't'.

The problem is that not everybody sees much in it for themselves; they go through the company conforming process, paying lip-service to a scheme whose benefits they have never been helped to appreciate. Undoubtedly in many organizations this process is actioned far more effectively in an informal gathering – perhaps a pub or outside of work altogether. It is so effective that frequently the target of the analysis does not even know that they have been evaluated or appraised.

It is not uncommon for the appraisal process to stop at the upper middle management of an organization, not getting to the top at all. It is no use convincing people who are trying to convince others that the company really believes in this, when it can be seen that most senior people don't take part. Other objections are that people say that the formulation of objectives is too mechanical and it's only possible for well-defined jobs such as the traditional widget maker.

OWNERSHIP

Appraisal schemes are seen to be owned by personnel departments; they supply the forms, look after them afterwards, and chase you if you don't do it. If more appraisal schemes were designed by, and became the property of, line managers and were used in the line management process, then it would remove some of the sterile properties of those schemes. It might also provide us with ladders and ropes to climb up the organization to say, 'Let's use the appraisal to pass some of your ideas up to me and see what you have really been doing this year, what you could have been doing and what you ought really to be doing'. This would eliminate the highly bureaucratic, downward institutions they so often become. Appraisal schemes could become very effective channels of upward management in organizations and reinforce and endorse the process. But they seldom are.

REWARDS

Very few people in organizations perceive any rewards emerging from the appraisal system. Therefore they do it reluctantly. They do it poorly and, generally, they do it late. If a boss really believed that the appraisal process would help him produce a more effective management from an individual, then he would enter into it with the same spirit of gaining a psychological reward. That might be increased performance. If, on the other hand, the subordinate felt that a reward might be a fair hearing, or a chance to express an opinion, or to generate a counter option, then he or she would get a psychological reward from it. The reward does not have to have money attached. It might simply be the reward of carrying out a job well for a change and seeing the value of it. There are very few organizations which reward managers or subordinates within the appraisal process properly, therefore it is carried out in the spirit of willing routine and expected to achieve nothing.

There is an issue called negative reward. If you do the appraisal properly, on time, and return the forms to the personnel department, then they don't nag you. This is hardly the spirit to encourage an open flow of ideas upwards into an organization, through a well drilled process.

NEW VERSUS OLD

The trouble is that most people have had bad experiences of appraisal and expect the one that is being revamped or reintroduced to be bad again. You could target your appraisal process specifically to encourage upward management. You could use it, say, to develop a set of options around objectives. Then we can choose the one that seems most likely and monitor performance against it. You choose the ways in which you will carry out the achievement of the objectives we have stated. In terms of managing upwards, it would take so little in the way of performance or attitude to make this a positive energy interchange and yet it seems to be flat and dull on so many occasions.

Unfortunately, the conventional wisdom of appraisal asks managers to behave in a way that is different from their usual behaviour and also from the way that their organization praises them for achieving bottom lines. Managers who are highly structured, who know where they are going, who direct peoples' thoughts into step-by-step directive thinking and directive results, are not the most comfortable in the open-ended situation of an appraisal. Feedback can be messy. It can stand in the way of action. It can generate a set of unwelcome and complicated alternatives. It can take control away from the manager who frequently is praised and rewarded for being action orientated. Finally, it does not involve action. 'It entails doing nothing and sitting around talking when we could be doing other tasks.' Appraisals are therefore perceived by many managers as having no value for them.

CONTEXT AND PERFORMANCE

One of the problems with appraisals is that they are often taken out of an organizational context and they reflect upon the individuals as if they were in no organization. For instance, one of the reasons why people may fail to achieve objectives is because they simply couldn't do it anyway. The truth may well be that something has occurred in the organization, since the objectives were set, that makes it completely impossible for people to achieve them. It is also possible for people to achieve objectives, or appear to achieve them, by a combination of luck and other peoples' efforts and so they are often taken out of context of organizations, which adds even more to their codification and coded language.

HELP

It is possible to reorientate the purpose and focus of your performance appraisal scheme to be far more closely linked to where your organization really works and also use it to promote concepts relating to upward management. It would be useful to be helped here. You could be helped by personnel departments, training or human resource departments. Tests and dummy runs could be of help but very seldom do personnel departments provide anything in the way of appraisal help. Their appraisal bureaucracy is usually seen as interfering and out of context with what really goes on in organizations.

There is sufficient written elsewhere on the subject of designing appraisal systems that is fair, useful and credible but so much of it appears to be written in code. A detailed explanation is given in *Practical Management Development* by Coates and Houchin. The important point is that appraisal systems should be centred on achieving objectives that are credible to both parties. This need for objectives not only gives a sense of purpose but also removes the problems of subjectivity and bias from the process.

SETTING OBJECTIVES

We need to determine briefly what is meant by an objective. There are many management dictionary definitions but we can make a definition that is probably simpler than most of those in textbooks and will be adequate for our purposes here: 'If I regard your performance as unsatisfactory and can describe what I have in mind as being a satisfactory performance, then what I describe as a satisfactory performance becomes an objective.'

In some (rare) circumstances an objective can be described very precisely and quantitatively. In most circumstances it can be defined quite precisely, with a few qualitative values included. The idea that all management action can be written down in terms of numbers or percentages is, I think, oversimplifying what is a difficult area.

The first priority is to come to an agreement on what performance should be, and we have to be careful that we move from poor performance to good performance in small steps. It may be that I would like my subordinate to be capable of running a large consultancy single-handed but for the moment I shall settle for her being able to handle the course papers for particular clients unaided by me and to get them right. Then we can go on to something much more clever.

The important point concerning objectives is that they are agreed by both parties and that they are clear enough to be evaluated. In other words, if I, the boss, and my appraisee agree that the objective was such and such and that we have not managed to meet it, or that the appraisee has not managed to meet it, then we can ask certain questions. If we have to argue: 'I think you didn't achieve it', 'I think I did', then we are going to find any kind of mutual evaluation difficult. It is rather like the accountancy term analysis of variance. At the end of a budget period the analysis of variance says: 'I set out to spend £10 000 on project A and in fact I spent £12,000 on it. The variance is £2,000. Why?'

We now come to the crux of this kind of objective-based performance appraisal system, if it works properly. If you can jointly set objectives and can jointly agree they have been met or not, then your appraisal system involves answering three key questions:

O   What did we set out to achieve and what really happened?
O   What do we learn from this?
O   What do we do next?

You could design your whole performance appraisal on a plain piece of paper and divide it into three sections which ask and answer those three questions.

Notice the use of the word 'we', especially in the second question, and that this question does not ask what training do you, or we, require. It says: What did we learn from this? What could the possible answers to this question be? We could learn, for instance, that our assumptions at the time of listing the objectives did not prove to be true; that something changed. We could learn that the subordinate didn't ask for help when it would have been appropriate, or that the boss promised help in engaging the assistance of another department but didn't do it as well as it could have been done. It could be that the subordinate was lazy. Perhaps the manager didn't delegate the work to the subordinate in the way that was previously agreed.

The answers and the questions are as long as you could imagine. What matters is to realize that performance is the result of a collaborative relationship between the manager and the managed. If your appraisal merely says 'You were wicked, you performed badly last year', then you are hardly likely to reach an upward flow of energy, or as we now style it – upward management. If your performance appraisal admits the possibility that we could learn from and act upon real actions, then you start to move into shared and collaborative management and the flow goes upward and, of course, downward. It is important to restate that upward management is not intended to replace downward management; it is intended to work with it.

There are some people for whom the performance appraisal

approach is too flexible and who feel uneasy when the simple, neat and quick approach of ticking boxes has been replaced with a less well-defined format. Let us go back to the issue called 'initiative'. Rather than rate your initiative on a scale from one to five, perhaps we could relate the abstract term 'initiative' to the analysis of variance of the objectives. For instance, it may well be that you have failed to achieve a particular agreed objective because you didn't use your initiative. You spotted an opportunity but didn't make the best use of it. It is perfectly realistic and fair to link the learning from achievement, or non-achievement, of objectives to making decisions about what needs to be done in the future. The question 'What did we learn?' allows this.

Another example would be the abstraction called 'judgement'. As a general rule I find it difficult to tick someone's judgement on a scale of one to five. However, I find that in dealing with that particular client, your judgement was absolutely spot on and that is what has allowed us to be successful in this case. So I am quite happy to talk about judgement and make comments about judgements in the context of particular, agreed management actions.

Thinking about appraisal in this way allows us to return to another theme. If you want to manage upwards you have to assert yourself. To assert yourself you have to have certain rights and one of these is knowing what is expected of you. This in turn leads to responsibilities and since we now have a process that contracts objectives between two people on a mutual basis, we can now say: 'We agreed to do certain things. You agreed to support me. Please do it', or 'We agreed certain things. You agreed that I could get some training in this area. You are not arranging it.'

The mutual contract allows the right for upward management. It also assigns responsibility to the upward manager and it makes criticism a very much easier task. For example, you have agreed that a project would be completed by the end of the year and in this case, you are the appraisee. Certain plans and timescales are implicit in the achievement of that objective and if, at the halfway point, you have agreed to be in a particular position and you are not, your boss may criticize your work on the basis of pre-agreed plans and objectives. You may also refute this criticism on the same basis. Having jointly agreed objectives allows a much more open type of management confrontation, based on pre-agreements rather than instant reactions.

PERFORMANCE MANAGEMENT SYSTEMS

There is a movement away from managers being regarded as custodians of appraisal schemes to becoming managers who are responsible for enhancing the performance of the people who work for them. This shifts the emphasis from being the steward of a bureaucratic system to being part of a system that adds value to the work of the organization.

We are hearing more about performance management, which looks at culture and strategy and autonomy in management, and the following example from a leading US retailer shows the steps in a performance management system. (Notice the names attached to players.) The scheme involves a manager and an associate.

Issue	Who?
What is my part in the key things we want to achieve?	Associate
What are the best ways of getting my associate to accomplish what the strategy requires of them?	Manager
How far can I go? What is my authority?	Associate
How are you doing? How are we doing? You tell me and I'll tell you	Both
What progress are we making on the key strategic tasks?	Both
Good job. Let's celebrate!	Both
What do you need now to do bigger and better things?	Manager

I am sure that much of this happens informally in many organizations. How much better it would be if this kind of thinking was formally incorporated into appraisal and not just left to chance. A particularly useful book which looks at this kind of approach is *Adding Value* by Gerald Egan.

6

WHY MANAGE UPWARDS?

❖

By now it is probable that you will have some questions for which you would like answers. So the purpose of this chapter is to pose and answer these questions, some of which are quite difficult. For instance, if you want to start to manage upwards is it simply a matter of good intentions and good communication or does someone have to create structural or organizational change to support it? .

WHAT RISKS DO YOU TAKE IF YOU TRY TO MANAGE UPWARDS IN AN ORGANIZATION?

As with any process new to the organization, there will be difficulties in starting to manage upwards. These may not necessarily be the same as risks. If you are perceived as cheeky and aggressive and anarchic, then your chances of developing a system where managing upwards will succeed will be slim.

On the other hand, you may wish that the staff who report to you were more competent in managing upward processes. It is unlikely that you will be at the end of a management chain but are almost certainly in the middle of it. If you are at the bottom of the management structure, the lowest supervisory manager, you may have no one who you wish to encourage to manage upwards to you or, if you are at the top of the organization, managing upwards to your own Board or steering committee may be an odd process.

It is a paradox but if you want to make managing upwards completely risk free, you automatically stifle the whole process because if you won't or can't do it, your staff can't do it to you.

IF YOU TRY TO MANAGE UPWARDS IN A TRADITIONALLY DOWNWARD ORGANIZATION, WHAT PROBLEMS WILL YOU HAVE?

If yours is a long-established organization, built around a downward power flow and a role culture, then managing upwards is going to be more difficult. But there is every indication that these types of organizations are decreasing in number.

Current thinking on management issues is polarized to two extreme viewpoints: the 'chaos' theory – that everything is in free fall and is freely available; or the need to return to a formal bureaucracy and hierarchy. As in most cases, there is probably a middle route that values and structures upward and downward energies in organizations. For instance, many of the traditional primary conversion industries, such as cement making, coal mining, steel making, which were very good examples of downward management in organizations, have largely disappeared, or the technology has changed so much that the 'we own you; we have power over you' culture has gone for ever. But what will replace it?

Banking is a good example of an industry trying to transform itself from a Victorian middle-class preserve into a modern enterprise that serves its customers. But if that is what you wanted to design from the outset, would you really start with those huge complicated buildings and male 'we know best' culture? The trouble with change is that you have to start from where you are; we get very few chances to start again from scratch.

You are not trying at first to change the whole organization. You are trying to change and improve the relationship you have with your boss and, in turn, to be a better boss to the people you manage. You don't need a corporate blessing for this kind of activity. If you do it properly it won't be apparent on the outside anyway but the benefits internally will be enormous.

It is interesting to examine the changing traditions in organizations and society over the past 50 years. With few exceptions we have only had management books since the Second World War. Most of these have appeared in the last 20 years. The most widely read and popular ones have only been with us for the last ten years. They examine organizations and management, and authority and structures. During these forty years, the society in which these managed enterprises exist has changed immensely.

Consider the way people communicate with one another, how they dress when they have the choice and the way that things happen in an apparently haphazard way but happen none the less. The society which these enterprises serve is changing. Therefore their customers are changing and their human raw material, which comes from that society, is changing.

The traditional Edwardian authoritarian family has changed. Some people regret its passing but it has changed. Children are encouraged to become part of the decision-making fabric of the family. Many children no longer go to school in uniforms, yet we still dress up in our uniforms to go to work. All the distinctions of hierarchy that were acceptable 20, and certainly 40, years ago are changing and we have to assume that they will continue to do so.

Many aspects have changed. Take authority, for instance. Once upon a time, if your boss said 'do this' you did it, it didn't matter what 'it' was. Authority went with the job, like a uniform, and the boss called you Coates, not Mr Coates. No wonder that managers who have been brought up like that by their bosses find it worrying when their authority is tested and challenged: 'Could I just finish this first? I'm finding it very interesting.'

It hardly seems fair. You are 'in authority' to your boss but these newcomers don't want to take it. And who are they anyway, these new starters with their strange, casual way of dressing and behaving? In many cases they are the contemporaries of your children who you encouraged to challenge their teachers, to use their initiative, not to accept all they are told, to stand on their own two feet. Once managers were people who 'know how things are done here'. Now it seems much less obvious.

Upward management concerns recognizing that this conflict is the way we are evolving and unless a very strange event happens, it is the way we are going to continue to evolve. Upward management using initiative, gently challenging, even joking and debunking of the boss is something we recognise in our activities outside of work.

There is plenty of evidence of people with great energy, management skill and authority which they apply in their private activities but which they leave behind in the lobby as they come to work, hanging it up with their coat. Examples of this might include bringing up a family; being actively involved in a club, a church or a charity; campaigning in a fund-raising appeal. To unleash that energy, imagination and creativity in some purposeful and coherent way would make organizations richer and more successful. Richness is not only measured in terms of money.

Sometimes we discuss management and management activity inside organizations in terms of energy flow. We imagine stifled organizations where the energy has long since leaked out. When we think of upward management we see huge bursts of energy rising, in a controlled and purposeful way, from the core up to the senior managers providing them with ideas, options and possibilities.

DOES MANAGING UPWARD MEAN MORE WORK FOR ME?

Well yes, it might and if that work made your organization stronger and more successful, more adaptable to change and more capable of being competitive, wouldn't that additional work be worth while? If the alternative to not taking on more work is to see your organization fail to take advantage of the benefits of upward management, then the organization will suffer and so will you. If some of the organizations in the UK that experienced difficulties in the early 1990s had been able to make use of their younger middle management talent, it is possible that they might not be in their current position.

If you feel that work has to be defined by the rule book, or by the job description, then upward management may strike you as rather an effort. If so you may be happier to work on a command basis and vent your frustration on the rule book when you don't accomplish your objectives.

ISN'T MANAGING UPWARDS JUST A NEW WORD FOR DELEGATION?

If delegation works successfully, junior managers in the hierarchy are asked – or empowered – to undertake tasks that previously they might not have been able or thought it possible to do. Currently, much is written about the notion of empowering, some of it slightly insulting. 'Go on, I empower you!' Surely that is the essential part of management. It seems patronizing but this depends on the initiative of the upper manager in making the process work and there are all sorts of reasons why people will not – or cannot – delegate. Managers are often nervous about letting go. Only their standards are sufficient. How will they be able to be sure that the risk involved in delegation will be minimized, or even non-existent?

Delegation stems from the upper manager. It is a consequence of power downward management. Upward management stems from the lower manager who sees the possibilities for change that she, or he, could and probably should make. (There are legitimate reasons why the boss may not have noticed them or may not have realized their importance.) He or she doesn't say, 'What about my doing this?' or 'Something needs to be done about this' or 'Its always bad. This is another example'. Instead, they think their ideas through, structure them, generate options and offer the benefits of the most suitable option and, using some of the communication skills we have discussed (and will discuss further in Chapter 8), presents them to the upper manager. The final result may be the same and in an organization where the practice of delegation is well-established and there are no errors over such matters as poor timing, or confused instructions, it might be far less necessary to involve upward management.

Timing is important here. The delegating manager wishes a piece of work to be done by the associate manager but with all sorts of pressure at the time, he forgets to pass on the message or command until its already rather late and thus creates enormous problems in the work of the delegated manager. As we have already seen, this is a process frequently caused by carelessness rather than malice. If the upward manager is more prepared to seek out opportunities to clarify and even reconsider timescales, to recognize that even a delayed timescale which will cause him problems might still be renegotiated, then the management process is far more healthy and assertive. We are so steeped in a culture that assumes the boss is right that we don't seek to check out whether or not it is true. It is not anarchy. It is positive and helpful.

We are, however, led to the idea that the word 'delegating' (downward) does not have a sufficiently well-defined meaning to distinguish it from the words 'upward management', so, perhaps we could use the phrase coined by Tadashi Kume at Honda, 'upward-downward'. Maybe we should recognize that we should use the notion of upward-downward management more often as a way of describing more usefully and precisely the energy flows between managers and managed. Isn't the issue of managing across and sideways just the same?

Managing across, not just to colleagues within the organization but to departments within the organization where we have no internal hierarchical connection and external organizations, are obviously very important. It is not satisfactory for a manager to say: 'I failed to achieve this project because I could not get the co-operation of another manager in the department, whose help I needed but there was no way that I could tell him to do things.' Influencing skills are useful upwards and are inevitable and important sideways and downwards.

We have seen that there are organizations which have made structural adjustments and adaptations to harness the energies of managers in the middle of the organization, but it is possible to achieve an improvement in managerial effectiveness without these structural adjustments. You can almost feel the potency of the energy being released in those organizations that set out to do it but it can also be achieved by small work groups within large enterprises.

7

MAKING IT HAPPEN

❖

If having read this far you think that you would like to perform better as an upward manager then you need to understand two issues. The first is change, in the sense that you are moving from a former behaviour which you want to modify, to a more interesting or useful form of behaviour. The second is learning. You are going to need to learn in a new and different way in order to behave effectively. Change and learning in this case are completely interlinked and in this chapter we look at how you learn and at the same time bring about the change you want. To do this I shall introduce you to the 'Learning River'.

People sometimes fail to understand why learning is so important to personal change. Quite simply, if you are trying to do something new that you didn't or couldn't do before then you have to learn it. The learning process might be long or short, simple or difficult, but it has to take place. It will not happen automatically. The Learning River asks managers to think out exactly what they want to achieve and what changes they need to make. Then it looks at all the possible ways of achieving this and what and how they need to learn.

The Learning River evolved out of some work that my company did to help an organization to work out what it wanted from its management development programme. It is now being used widely by managers to plan the steps in the learning processes they need. Before describing the Learning River it is important to know a theory set out by Reg Revans in his ideas on action learning. Revans states that learning, L, is the sum of two components, P and Q. In other words $L = P + Q$.

P learning stands for programme, or programmed learning, and relates to all of those skills you can learn on a course, or by following a package. It could be an accountancy course, an Open University course, a weekend course in computer programming; there are many courses, or packages, available which help us to learn these skills. You choose a course, or a package, because you have respect for the wisdom of the author, or the authors. And people who make packages, or programmes, usually have considerable experience and often have interesting ideas and interpretations. In a sense this book is a programme. The problem with programmes, and the problem with this book, is that it knows nothing about the person reading it. Although it may be making interesting comments about organizations, it doesn't know about you, your boss, your organization, your difficult situations, your difficult customers or the advantages and disadvantages of working in the culture of your organization. How could it?

Q learning stands for questioning. It refers to all those matters that we frequently wonder about in the workplace and that are unique to our work situation and work. Typical Q questions are:

○   Why do we do it this way? Why do we do it at all?
○   How long have we been doing that? Isn't there a better way?
○   I wonder why we tolerate that problem instead of trying to solve it?
○   I wonder why we put up with that kind of production system even though we know it doesn't work?
○   What problems hold up progress in this organization because they are regarded as undiscussable?
○   Why do I find it hard to influence Peter but not Gillian?

It is important to remember that neither P nor Q is better, they are two components in learning, especially in learning about management. There is a place for P programmes and there is a place for Q questioning and observation in the workplace. We know, however, that P learning is generally regarded as 'safe'. It takes place in a business school, in a university, in a hotel, on someone else's premises. Whereas Q learning is often confrontational and challenging in the workplace. P learning is often private, Q learning involves colleagues, both upwards and downwards. If you are to make progress in managing upwards you are going to have to tackle a number of issues and learn from them and some of them may not be completely enjoyable. If you try to introduce a new way of working into your organization it may well be that you can benefit personally by some P learning but the implementation of that learning in the workplace is going to require a number of issues called Q.

With this theory in the back of our minds we tried to think through, with our client, the design of their management development programme. We produced for them a series of short modules, typically lasting two or three days, typically separated by six to eight weeks in the workplace. Our hope was that they would return to work and apply, or observe, the ideas that they had been thinking through and discussing in the classroom. It became evident that this was not the case and that they regarded the learning process as occuring exclusively when they were in the training centre with us and they did not regard their time at work as an equivalent learning process.

We sought an analogy to explain that they were involved in a complete learning process, both at work and away from work in the conference centre. We hit on the idea of a river which starts its life in a bubbly and unformed way, often changing direction, gradually becoming more settled in its path and more predictable, being joined by other rivers, sometimes going through long, straight, stretches when cruising is enjoyable and sometimes going through very difficult patches of broken white water, finally arriving at what we call 'the port of destination'. Managing in an organization involves completing a succession of learning rivers, starting at a new starting point and finishing at yet another new port of destination (see Figures 7.1 and 7.2).

The port of destination is important. We need the learning to be seen as helping a manager to arrive somewhere; to really achieve goals. The last thing we want is for busy managers to feel that planning learning is selecting courses from a catalogue. Typical ports of destination might be:

O   opening a new branch
O   launching a new product
O   chairing the committee
O   handing over this part of my job to Jean
O   reducing the management layers in a department
O   effectively managing upwards.

In the life of a normal, busy manager there is very little time to get out of the river and discuss theories, concepts and new ideas. We call stopping off at islands in the river 'stopping at P islands'. Learning from struggling down the river, sometimes finding life interesting and sometimes finding life difficult, we call Q learning. So the Learning River is a continuous picture, perhaps lasting six, nine, or 12 months, with a fixed starting point 'Here I am today' and with a fixed ending point 'This is what I want to be doing at a certain date'. It also maps out some of the events that may happen along the way.

Not only do you find P islands in the Learning River but you find there are other people in the organization who have an interest either in promoting the change process, or preventing it. In the Learning River there are pilots, who are there to help you learn more effectively. Pilots may be colleagues, they may be bosses, they may be the training department, they may be mentors, they may be spouses. But there are also pirates, and crocodiles and white water. Pirates are visible, there to prevent you achieving what you want to achieve. Your achievement will be a threat to their *status quo* and they will plan to weaken your approach. Crocodiles are more insidious because they are not visible and sometimes even calm, peaceful and empty stretches of wide water may contain crocodiles.

Where is the white water in the workplace? White water represents turbulent times and these sometimes make managers increasingly anxious and even stressed as they can see the turbulence coming. Typical examples of organizational turbulence might be the launch of a new product, the merger of two departments, the departure of a well-liked boss, and these can be anticipated and planned for. Sometimes they come on you as a complete surprise.

How you cope with white water or turbulence in the workplace depends on your particular approach to learning. Individuals have

Figure 7.1   The Learning River

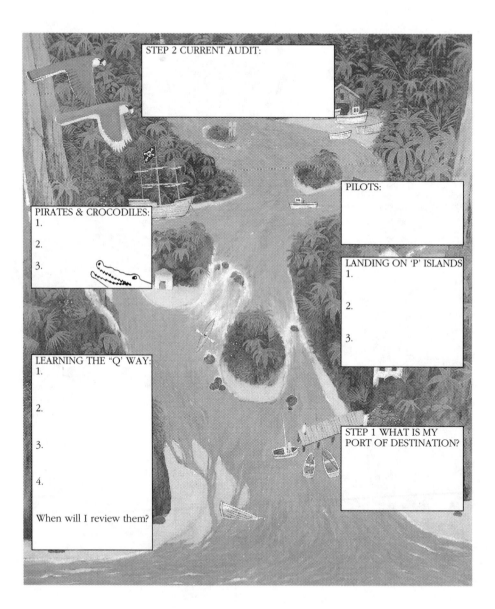

Figure 7.2   The Learning River plan

different learning styles and preferences and your approach to learning in difficult times will depend upon these. You may quite happily just hurl yourself down the river and see what happens and say 'Gosh! that was fun' or 'Gosh! that was awful'. You may sit on the bank watching other people, thinking carefully about what is happening to them and see what you can learn from that. You may go on a training course called 'How to navigate in white water', or go along with someone else who shows you what to do, is prepared to come down the water with you and tries to be of help. Readers who know the Honey and Mumford learning styles (from *Using Your Learning Styles*) will recognize that the four styles correspond to these.

The Learning River recognizes that most of the learning you will do will be in the workplace, from the experiences you have in the workplace – if you learn from them. In this particular situation it is probable that the learner will be trying to do something new in a familiar situation in his or her own workplace. Clearly there are opportunities to learn by working in completely different environments but if we are learning to manage upwards in our own organization, the environment stays the same, it is the behaviour that has to change.

Q learning, or learning from experience, sounds simple. People talk about learning from experience, or learning from the school of life, or the school of hard knocks and it is noticeable that although people have experiences they don't learn from them. You have only to drive down a motorway to see that there are people driving who have been doing it for twenty years but in that time they haven't learned anything at all, or they haven't learned anything very beneficial. I find that managers often arrive at experiences in a rather random, or unplanned way and even when they succeed they don't always learn from the experience. The whole purpose of action learning as a way of developing managers is to get them to plan the experiences they want and then to help them to learn from them.

You might imagine that people are constantly planning experiences to learn from and then, having had the experience, they learn from it. Sadly it isn't true: people have experiences but these are the ones that the job throws at them and only in-frequently do they learn from them. Q learning in a real environment requires managers not only to intend to seek out certain experiences but also to take time to learn from them. This time normally has to be fought for: it is not normally there unless you make it happen.

Recently my company was asked by an organization to help them develop their influencing and negotiating skills for some work they were doing with the EC in Brussels. We agreed that we could give them a one- or two-day short course in negotiating but we felt that would probably not address the things that they were experiencing in the conference rooms of Brussels and Strasbourg. We offered instead to meet the managers involved with these negotiations on a one-day-a-quarter basis, shortly after each negotiation had taken place. It was suggested that they did this anyway. That after every meeting they should sit down and analyse what had happened, for good and for bad. The truth is, however, that they did not want to meet and talk about them; they have busy workloads, they have full in-trays and they go back to work.

We met with this group three times and addressed issues such as: what was going well until it started to go off the rails? Whose behaviour upset you? Where were you unprepared? After three meetings the team were beginning to win in their particular negotiating positions in the EC. Is this just luck, the fact that we make people sit down and talk them through experiences that they perhaps wished that they weren't reliving. The basis of Q learning requires structure and planning and merely to rely on random experiences and poor learning processes is not what is meant by learning from experience.

So much then for the theory of the Learning River. How can we understand better how a manager might make use of its ideas and its disciplines to become a more effective upward manager? This is after all the purpose of this book. The case history which follows shows in detail the planning process used by a manger who wanted to have more influence in the managing upwards process. We see how this manager planned the learning and change strategies which she felt she needed and we see over the course of the year how she succeeded and how she learned.

THE STORY OF SELINA HEWITT

Selina Hewitt is 31 years old and works for a large British bank. She is a history graduate of Hull University and joined the bank eight years ago after a one year voluntary assignment in Nigeria helping to organize a rural travelling library. By the standards of the bank, to be promoted to manager at 31 is a good performance. Her boss in the Product Development Division is Ralph Hopkins. The purpose of the division is to investigate potentially marketable banking products and instruments, to research the market and to launch prototype and pilot products into the market-place. At a time of recession and increased competition between banks there is a constant tension between the introduction of new products and the marketing and business development of existing ones. New products are not always well received in the banking structure itself.

Selina has two colleagues at her level, both men, and she in turn manages five supervisors. She was promoted exactly one year ago from being a supervisor herself. Selina has for some time realized that, although she has a good relationship with Ralph Hopkins, they could improve it if he allowed her to have more input into the partnership. She feels that she has much more to offer than she is currently giving but is not sure whether this feeling stems more from her ideas or those of her boss. She feels that their working relationship could be improved.

So Selina decides to complete the Learning River and this is the way her thinking develops. First of all she identifies that she has two ports of destination; one is with her boss, surrounding the issue of being able to manage upwards more; and the other is with her staff, encouraging them to manage upwards to her. She realizes that she cannot just intend to manage upwards more herself without making it something for her staff to aim for as well.

Selina has great difficulty describing the port of destination and she gives herself one year for this river journey. A problem arises in that it is not a simple question of setting a neat objective but there are many descriptions and outcomes that she wants to achieve. For instance, if she considers the port of destination called 'with my boss' Selina would have to:

○   take responsibility for many more management issues

○   have less misunderstanding between her and her boss, fewer last minute crises and, probably, a greater workload for her herself

○   be more helpful in formulating possible new approaches to familiar problems. She feels that they all tend to follow the same sort of approaches to problems rather than generate a wider range of options and choices. She recognizes that this is an area where Ralph will not agree easily. Many of the well-tested approaches are his and have been so for some time

○   be part of a dual relationship where Selina is more valued as a manager and more influential than she is now. She feels that she is valued for her technical, especially her market research, skills but not her skills as a manager. She feels that sometimes her boss goes directly to her own staff and she would like this to stop

○   take more responsibility for achieving things herself and with her team.

This is a good picture of a port of destination. It is not simple but it does give a well-defined sense of direction. In contemplating the port of destination that she wishes to gain with her staff, she wants them to be coming to her with specific ideas which are well worked through for her approval. She wants the team to have respect for themselves and therefore not only to go to her with completed ideas but to work them out with one another. She needs to value them for their management skills and efforts and realizes that some of them, although they have quite strong personalities, have poorly developed management skills. She needs them to help her by appraising upwards and examine her management styles and effectiveness.

Selina carries out a SWOT analysis on her own personal performance and achievement:

○   Strengths
       good technical skills
       good at finishing things off
       enthusiastic
       well organized

well abreast of current market research techniques
○ Weaknesses
I frequently know what I want to do and start doing it without telling anyone
I don't particularly like being supervised and don't feel that I am always the best person to be managed by somebody else
I don't suffer fools gladly and I am not sure whether this is the best role for me in the organization; I feel it is too much of a back-room role and I would like to be out in a more up-front position.
I know that this particular post is a recognizable one, however, where if I could do well and conform to what the bank wants, then I will be recognized.
○ Opportunities
the bank's new approach to total quality programmes
there are new opportunities on the international side in East Europe and Russia and I have an ambitious boss, which might mean that I can take advantage of this in my work
○ Threats
a general recession is causing a slow down in business activity
there have been branch closures
market research is seen as an expensive luxury.

Selina now tries to connect the current audit with the port, or ports, of destination and recognizes first of all there is no P course called 'managing upwards', although she could probably benefit – in her port of destination with her boss – from some better influencing and assertiveness skills. She also recognizes that some of her own staff may benefit from a suitable basic management course but she doesn't want it to be too theoretical and would like them to be helped and encouraged to put the learning into practice when they return to work.

As far as Q learning is concerned, Selina realizes that there needs to be a great deal of experimentation and review and that these experiments will not always work out. She plans to meet with her team on one afternoon a month for the whole year to review their own effectiveness in learning to manage upwards, but she is not sure how to approach her boss with this. She decides that the initial approach ought to be to put it in writing to him – this is a valid approach – and then to go and talk to him about it. She is a bit fearful about his reaction to her managing upwards, especially as she is a woman. Many women in the bank have done well but there is always an atmosphere of surprise or scepticism.

As far as pilots are concerned, Selina is unsure. She recognizes that her husband will be very supportive but she is not sure who in the bank might be a helper. She remembers that on a course two years ago she met a fairly senior manager, also a woman, with whom she became good friends. Although this woman doesn't work in her part of the bank, Selina wonders if it might be worth asking her how she might go about this kind of exercise.

As far as people who hinder the processes are concerned, Selina wonders how the two colleagues at her own level, both of whom are men, will take to this initiative. Might they see it as threatening? Will she be seen as manipulative and setting out to do something on her own, which will mark her out from the normal way managers are developed in this organization? This thinking allows Selina to devise a rough plan of learning and change for the next twelve months.

She asks the training department to find for her a short course on assertiveness. They suggest a three-day residential programme on assertiveness for senior women managers. Although she is at first a bit worried by the 'women' orientation, she enjoys the programme and feels she has benefited from it.

She certainly finds it easier now to challenge some of her own staff. One of them is very able but tends to behave in a rather passive way. Selina deals with this and by asking him to represent the department at an important meeting and specifically asking him to generate a number of possible solutions to the problem on the agenda of greatest importance to the department. He produces two ideas but Selina does not think that this is enough and asks him for more. He grudgingly produces another three and even more grudgingly puts together action plans that would, if necessary, support all five options.

In the event, the meeting seeks a new way of solving this kind of problem. It listens to all the normal ways and finally realizes that Selina's colleague has a new approach that not only appeals to them but also seems to have been well worked through. They decide to adopt this solution and ask him to tell Selina that they are pleased with this outcome. He feels rather proud and admits to her that the chosen solution was in fact the fourth option. They are both pleased. Selina has encouraged her colleague to greater productivity and he has produced a new but accepted approach.

Selina also goes on a short course on project management as she feels the need to be better organized and realizes that some of the techniques such as scheduling work flow can probably be explained quickly in a course. However, she has much to learn about her own approach to managing upwards that she will not find on a course.

Her research shows that the bank has fewer university student accounts than they would expect. She believes firmly that although these accounts sometimes pose problems to the bank, they are the market of the future and are worth promoting. She collects her data carefully and arranges a time for a presentation to Ralph in the knowledge that he can be cautious on this kind of issue and does not share her enthusiasm for students or their accounts. The presentation goes very well. The detailed argument shows the under-representation clearly. Ralph thanks her and takes her out to lunch. Nothing happens. A few weeks later Selina mentions the subject to Ralph who talks enthusiastically but also talks about 'other priorities'. The idea dies.

Some time later, Selina's group raises the idea of a customer helpline or a help desk. Before she tries it on Ralph they look at all possible options and compare ways of achieving this and its costs. The group believe that the best way is on a regional basis so they run a minor trial in the north west area. It works well and Selina now presents it to Ralph, not simply as a statement of a problem but as a range of possibilities; the reasons for the one they propose; the results of the trials and a costed management structure for the implementation. They expect Ralph to be very pleased but on the contrary, he is very surprised that they have gone so far without letting him know. For the first time Ralph and Selina discuss their relationship in detail.

As he thinks more about what she has done, he realizes that what she is proposing is very important and gives it his blessing but asks her to involve him slightly earlier next time. His grapevine has thrown up some strange questions from colleagues in the north west who were obviously very nervous about Selina's trials. 'Who is that woman, anyway?' The discussion is very important to Selina. It also makes her realize where her student account ideas had gone; Ralph was not in a position to cope with 'raw, good ideas, however fascinating'.

Selina capitalizes on her success by making some changes to the way that her department is structured. She discusses it with her staff and then makes a summary proposal to Ralph on two pieces of paper, showing what she has in mind and offering to report progress in three months. He agrees promptly.

The relationship improves further and Ralph starts to talk openly to Selina about issues that are worrying to him. He opens up concerning the organization in a way that she had never imagined before. There is a rumour, he explains that their 'opposite number' department, Market Research, might be reduced or closed down. Discussing cost reduction is an everyday occurrence here.

In fact the department is not closed down but merged with Ralph's and for several months the whole pattern of work is chaotic and very stressful. There are now five managers reporting to Ralph, and Selina organizes an away weekend to teamwork with her new colleagues. She invites Ralph but he decides not to come until the final afternoon to allow them space to think without him. He asks to see the timetable, however, and asks them to include a session on stress with a speaker from outside. The meeting is a success and all the managers agree to hold a similar but non-residential meeting for their own teams.

At the end of the year Selina reviews her own learning objectives and feels certain that she is now managing upwards more effectively. She has learned that merely having good ideas can be seen at best as a nuisance and at worst as threatening. She has discovered that banks have vertical boundaries that respect status and horizontal boundaries that respect jobs. You can cross or bend boundaries but they are strong and you have to think carefully about how you do this. Work was always delegated to her but she now feels more important and more potent as a manager. She sees her relationship with Ralph as an upward-downward relationship.

8

THE SKILLS OF MANAGING UPWARDS

❖

We have seen that there are two main problems that have to be resolved in order to make the managing upwards process successful. The first one is an organizational one where the organization sees the value of tapping into management energy and allowing it to flow upwards. The second one is personal skills which involves the ability of individual managers to assert their views upwards.

MANY PEOPLE FIND IT DIFFICULT TO BE ASSERTIVE

Assertiveness can be confused with selfishness or aggressiveness; with putting our own needs before those of others and pursuing them regardless. This can be threatening and upsetting and is certainly not assertiveness. Assertiveness is recognizing our own needs and asking openly and directly for what we want. It is respecting and recognizing the needs and rights of other people. It is relating to people in personal and working situations in an open and honest way. It is taking responsibility for and keeping control over our actions. It is being able to resolve difficulties and disputes in a way that feels comfortable, fair and just to those involved. It is confronting issues in the workplace that appear to be ineffective or unfair. Assertiveness is not the same as aggressiveness. Aggressiveness is expressing feelings in a way that punishes, threatens, or puts other people down. It disregards the rights of others in the workplace and it aims to get our own way no matter what.

Non-assertive, submissive, or passive behaviour implies that we do not stand up for our rights and we allow others to take advantage of us. We avoid responsibility for making choices and leave others to make decisions for us; we are not in control of our lives or our work; we see ourselves as put-upon by other people and victims of unfair situations. Finally there is conduct which is known as 'being manipulative'. This is a form of behaviour which we see when people are unable to ask directly for what they want and they manoeuvre people by playing games, or making them feel guilty.

If we are going to behave as upward managers in an assertive way we need to recognize our own rights and the rights of others in the organization and express these rights in a way that is open and honest. Consider how you would respond to the following situations at the workplace:

O   you are criticized unjustly
O   your boss or someone you work with makes sexist remarks or harasses you in public
O   you have to confront someone who works for you who is continually late, sloppy, or dishonest
O   your boss asks you to do more than you feel is justified by the sort of job you hold
O   your boss takes your idea and promotes it as if it were her own
O   your boss praises your work or compliments you on your appearance
O   someone notices when you have worked well and made an extra effort
O   you have an important presentation to make to a group of senior managers and you have insufficient time to prepare.

How would you recognize assertive behaviour if you saw it? Assertive behaviour is based on genuine respect for self and others. It is authentic and thereby accepts positive and negative attitudes to the way people feel about various matters. It shows responsibility for choices and actions but doesn't necessarily have to take responsibility for everybody else. There should be a genuine depth and wealth of self-esteem; it is from this self-esteem that the assertion comes – people know how they stand and where they are valued. An assertive person responds honestly and openly to others and gives themselves credit for so doing.

ASSESSING YOUR OWN ASSERTIVENESS AS AN UPWARD MANAGER

Think of three occasions during the last week or so when you have been involved in working with your own manager.

Think of an occasion when you have responded to your manager in an aggressive way (or felt like responding in an aggressive way but managed not to). How did the situation come about. How did you feel about responding in the way you did. What would you need to do to respond in a more assertive way?

Think of an occasion when you behaved in a submissive way and gave in. What was the result of this behaviour, how did you feel as a result of behaving this way? What would you need to do in the future to behave in a more assertive way as an upward manager?

Think of a time when you asserted yourself upwardly as a manager. Describe the situation. How did you feel about this? How did your boss feel about this? What would you have to do to keep on behaving in this way. What are the benefits to you and your organization?

Take some time and think through your answers to these questions. What does it tell you? What do you learn? What more do you need to do. What do you need to work at?

REFUSING REQUESTS

In order to assert our rightful role as a manager and assert it upwards towards our boss we sometimes have to refuse requests. It is normally disastrous to use simple refusal words like 'I won't', or 'I shall not' on their own. This is seen as aggressive and unhelpful behaviour. You can use the word 'no' but you have to put it into a context.

There are some simple frameworks for refusing requests

assertively from a position of right, thereby maintaining the managing upward momentum.

O   Listen carefully to the point of view contained in the request.
O   Respond, keeping your reasons to a minimum but still being precise.
O   Maintain firm eye contact and a positive posture.
O   Use the word 'no' or a similar explicit refusal.
O   Repeat these steps where necessary.

An example:

> *'So you want me to give you a hand with this table, Dave. I can see what you're asking for but right now I am in the middle of something which is also important so I'll have to say, no.'*

Another example:

> *'Can you give me a report on this incident by tonight?'*

> Response: *'I realise it's important to you but I don't think it will be possible to give a full report by tonight. There's simply not enough time. I could give you a summary if that would be helpful'.*

And yet another example:

> *'Please can you stay late tonight and work; we've got a lot to do.'*

> Response: *'I realise that we've got problems with this extra work but I've agreed to go shopping with my daughter, so I will not be able to stay late. Will it help if I come in early in the morning and we make a very early start on it?'*

In all of these examples, the request is refused from a position of 'right', whether the right is a workplace derived right or a right from outside of the workplace. In every case the refuser recognizes the need of the requester and there is no aggression in having made the request, and no unreasonableness contained in the reply. Each reply contains an element of compromise or making suggestions that are intended to be specifically helpful.

COPING WITH CRITICISM

Being criticized is often regarded as stressful and that leads us to act defensively or aggressively, and this might weaken our positions as upward managers. Responding to criticism assertively helps you to distinguish valid from invalid criticism, discover things about yourself which may be affecting your relationship with your boss, and allows you to express your feelings.

Here is a structure for dealing with criticism.

O   Listen to the criticism
O   Give feedback showing that you have heard it
O   Agree or disagree - make a decision
O   State your feelings
O   Check it out.

For example

'Jonathan, you really got annoyed at yesterday's meeting didn't you?'

'You thought I was pretty angry about yesterday's meeting did you – well, yes I was. I had a lot of work on and we seemed to be going round and round getting nowhere. Did I cause problems for you?'

This accepts the criticism, realizes the implication of the criticism, which was perhaps not evident before, and honestly acknowledges that it might have caused problems.

Equally, we might have to express criticism, or doubt, about the efficiency, or effectiveness, of certain pieces of work upwards to our boss. This is particularly difficult and sometimes we don't know where to begin. It is only going to work if it is seen as specific, non-personal and identifies particular issues to do with improvement.

Similarly, offering praise or encouragement is as frequently poorly handled by downward managers as upward managers – it's often forgotten, or undervalued. Praise is normally offered on the successful completion of a task but encouragement can be given to colleagues, or bosses when matters aren't going so well. It is usually possible to find something positive in every undertaking, however small.

This framework will be helpful:

○   be specific and clear
○   don't be too expressive or overly demonstrative
○   keep it simple.

Example:

> *'I thought the way you put the presentation to the board this morning was very well prepared and professional. You should be very pleased.'*

Or even to the boss

> *'I hadn't realized just how tricky that client could be. I don't think I could have handled it the way you did.'*

or as a boss

> *'Generating so many new possible solutions to the problem gave us the opportunity to solve it in a new way. I like this way of working.'*

THE RIGHT TO BE ASSERTIVE

When we talk about being assertive and managing upwards we ask the question: 'What gives us the right to do this?" Of course, we should also ask the question: 'What gives our boss the right to manage in the way that he, or she, does?' But since our subject is managing upward; what gives us the right to be able to manage upward and to assert our professional and management ability on to that of our boss? Remember, that all power is not equally shared and therefore you may not always win arguments that you make in this way. Managing upwards is derived from rights and we have to look carefully at where we get our rights in the workplace.

Here are some of the issues involving rights and responsibilities at work.

○   I have the right to manage my time as effectively as possible.
○   I have the right to be informed about any decisions at work that will affect me, or my department.

○   I have the right to make mistakes from time to time because I recognize I am not always perfect.

○   I have the right to understand how my boss evaluates my performance.

○   I have the right to express concerns about work matters that I feel need to be discussed.

○   I have the right of veto, or discussion, about staff who may come to work for me.

○   I have the right to expect a certain standard of work and performance of the people I work with.

○   I have the right to refuse unreasonable requests.

As we have seen earlier, there are some responsibilities associated with these rights.

○   I have a responsibility for what happens as a result of what I do.

○   I have a responsibility to work with company policies and contracts, and so on.

○   I have a responsibility to respect the rights of others.

INFLUENCING OTHERS AT WORK (ESPECIALLY BOSSES)

We can start by saying that if people are different then we have to understand those differences and therefore influence them in different ways. There are many models of behaviour and preferences we could use to describe differences. The one we will use here comes from the work of Charles Margerison and Dick McCann who have developed a model which shows how people prefer to work when they are in teams. Since my boss and I are a team (of two) then we will find this approach helpful.

The real model of Margerison and McCann looks at eight types of people and the way they prefer to work. You can read all about it in Dick McCann's book *How to Influence Others at Work*. For now we are going to simplify this into a four way model: explorers, organizers, controllers and advisers.

EXPLORERS – ORGANIZERS – CONTROLLERS – ADVISERS

Explorers tend to be outgoing and strong. They can see the future. They may not be basically creative but they can take ideas and sell them to people in the organization. They thrive on possibilities; if you ask them for the basis of their ideas they can't always identify the source exactly. Sometimes it almost seems as though they make things up. You might be one of these. So might your boss.

Organizers are analytical and practical. They get things started. They make plans and timescales. They can be relied on to make things happen. They move on just enough information. When they are accused of not listening they point out that someone has to make things work round here. They are exceptionally useful and productive people. You might be one of these. So might your boss.

Controllers are down to earth and often rather quiet. They like quality control and audit work. They are rooted in reality. They are concerned with what happened; the facts. They are precise and insist on receiving hard data. They get nervous when people ask them to project the future and speculate on possibilities. You might be one of these and so might your boss.

Finally, advisers do just that. They advise. They are not impressed by people who have to rush into action. They like to research and gather their data carefully and if a new line of enquiry presents itself they will follow it. They are good at generating options and often hold strong and tested values on the ways things need to be done. They will not support hurried change or even change for change's sake. You might be one of these and so might your boss.

All of these managers exist. You are certainly one. If your boss is the same you will understand them but you might need to compete with them. If your boss is different you may well be in conflict.

Explorers are always looking to the future. Controllers are looking to the past 'what did we do?' Organizers are always moving into action. Advisers are often searching for more data. People have a right to prefer the way they work. What is your own preference? How do you influence someone who is different from you?

Dick McCann calls the process of influencing other sorts of people 'pacing'. We now consider pacing other people. If you are going to try and influence your manager in an upward way and you can make a crude assessment of the kind of behaviour he or she shows that would locate them in one of the above four categories then you can use different influencing strategies, depending on the sort of person they are.

This is a conversation between two managers in a small management training consulting organization. Joe is the managing director who founded the company. Carol is a fairly junior consultant who is known to be full of ideas.

CAROL: Joe, can I just have a few minutes? It's about an idea I've had for a new course.

JOE: Well its not really a very good time. I'm trying to put in all the project coding and schedules. But if it's just a minute . . . what is it?

CAROL: I've had this idea where we could add a day to our influencing skills course and get some real clients in for the learners to try to influence. This would do away with the need for those role plays which everyone finds uncomfortable and would add to the reality of it all. We all discussed this on my action learning Masters course and we . . ..

JOE: Hang on Carol! This sounds like another of your crazy ideas. This company has a good reputation for providing well tried and tested products and there's absolutely no need to go round trying to invent new aspects we don't need.

CAROL: But we do need it. Everyone says that the role-play approach doesn't deal sufficiently with the reality of interactions. They say that it limits the possibility of entering sensitive areas around client boundaries.

JOE: What do you mean everybody says. I'd like to know who everybody is.

CAROL: Well er . . . well there's um . . ..

JOE: See there you are. It is another of your scatty ideas. Quite frankly I'm worried about you Carol, always bringing me new ideas in a half-formed way and never doing the work we want you to do; like course evaluation reports

for instance. I haven't seen yours for the last three
weeks. Where are they?

CAROL: Yes I keep meaning to get down to those but surely we
have to keep thinking creatively about what is possible
or improvable and . . .

JOE: This is enough. You can't run a business like this with
half-formed ideas. And I decide on improvements.
Anyway I'm very busy. Now please go and turn your
attention to those course evaluation forms. I want them
by the end of the afternoon.

A sad conversation! Carol has not persuaded her boss of her idea's
value. She is failing to manage upwards because she is not
thinking how he is best influenced. In the four definitions we have
considered it seems that Joe is probably a Controller and Carol is
probably an Explorer.

How can you influence a Controller to accept your ideas?
Remember what they like. They like facts and order. They like
precision. They become nervous and flustered when presented
with what they regard as wild possibilities. So Carol would have
been smarter if she had done some of these things:

O   booked a precise time to see Joe, not just called in
O   put her ideas in writing beforehand
O   shown from her analysis of the course evaluations that
people are not very happy about the current way of role-
playing (she might as well turn Joe's prized evaluations to
her own advantage)
O   she could have given an example of it working in practice.

Of course Joe could have been more sympathetic to Carol's
exploring style but that is not the question here. Carol might find
it uncomfortable, even irritating, to pace Joe in this way but it
would certainly make her managing upward attempts more likely
to succeed.

Here are some general ideas about how you can influence
different types of people by playing to their preferences.

Explorers prefer and respond well to:
O   Opportunities to explore ideas
O   people who are enthusiastic

O   people who know what they are talking about and have a
         strong grasp of concepts
O   opportunities simply to talk
O   discussions which concentrate on possibilities and the
         future

Explorers dislike and respond negatively to:
O   excessive structure
O   tight or unreasonable deadlines
O   convergent, step-by-step thinking
O   situations where they are continually challenged about their
         opinions
O   discussions which concentrate on the past.

Organizers respond well to:
O   goals, targets and incentives
O   deadlines, milestones and people who are punctual
O   managers and subordinates who are well prepared
O   situations and subjects which have been well or fully
         analysed
O   discussions which focus on the facts
O   communications which are clear, logical and precise
O   progress reports and action summaries.

Organizers respond negatively to:
O   people who give their opinions and not the facts
O   people or situations which are speculative or vague
O   actions which do not produce a result or which waste their
         time
O   people who always want more time to think through other
         ways.

Controllers prefer and respond well to:
O   written communications, memos and formal agendas
O   people who reduce ideas to a system of step-by-step
         processes
O   people who think before they speak
O   managers who pay attention to detail
O   people who have 'done their homework'
O   practical people
O   communications which are clear and precise.

Controllers dislike and respond negatively to:
O   people who 'drop in on them' unexpectedly
O   surprises
O   managers who like change for its own sake
O   people who dominate discussions.

Advisers prefer and respond well to:
O   flexible approaches
O   people who emphasize personal relationships
O   co-operation rather than confrontation
O   people who welcome options.

Advisers dislike and respond negatively to:
O   environments which emphasize facts at the expense of feelings
O   occasions where they are rushed and feel inadequately informed
O   Situations where their basic beliefs are ignored.

What does your boss appear to be? What is her, or his, preference at work? How can you influence them through their strengths? How can you avoid approaching them in a way that threatens, cramps or simply irritates them?

PUSH AND PULL STYLES OF INFLUENCING

Much has been written about influencing styles. A useful distinction is between the use of 'push' or 'pull'.

Push influence style is characterized by having ideas and persistently proposing them and shutting out other ideas. It requires you to have numerous ideas: 'In my last company it always worked like this but this is another way we can do it.' It offers many alternatives: 'We can do it this way, or this or this. A better idea is this.' It proposes solutions: 'This is what we are going to do . . . . What you need is the 560SX machine.' It blocks out other people in your enthusiasm: 'Yes but this idea works, theirs might not. . . . No don't stop me I haven't finished. What I must say is . . . .'

PULL influence style is characterized by asking lots of questions and testing understanding and agreement. It requires you to ask questions regularly: 'Why do you think that? Is that what you believe?' It tests out understanding: 'I think from what you are saying you want us to . . .? What is your opinion so far?' It repeats, or paraphrases what they have said: 'So, if I have understood, you are anxious about this. So your need is for a programme for the Top Team?'

NEITHER IS RIGHT OR WRONG

To be successful you will have to try both strategies. But you have to know when to push and when to pull. If you are being asked for ideas you push. If you are trying to work out why it all went wrong last time you pull. If you are not quite sure where your power base lies you need to pull and explore gently. The secret is to pull to find out what is happening and obtain a real hearing. Then you might be able to push some of your ideas and solutions.

In the meeting between Carol and Joe, Carol would have done better to pull Joe to find out his views on the importance of the data she has gathered from the evaluation forms concerning the value of simulated role plays. She might even have asked Joe if he would like to hear about an idea that she had. Then, and only then, can she push Joe towards her ideas. It might take time and it does need skill.

SUMMARY

This chapter can only present some basic ideas on influencing. The important idea is to try and see matters through other people's eyes. How do they like to make decisions? How do they like ideas put to them? What makes them receptive? You can read more widely on this subject. We have already mentioned Dick McCann's book. You might find useful a book on assertiveness such as Ken and Kate Back's *Assertiveness at Work*. But the best way is to remember some of the lessons of Chapter 7 and the experiences of Selina Hewitt. Learn to experiment with your boss or bosses. Think about what works and what doesn't work. Learn from your real experiences to MANAGE UPWARDS!

RECOMMENDED READING

❖

In writing *Managing Upwards* I have deliberately tried to avoid re-presenting too much of the available wisdom of management either by rewriting it all or by listing an exhaustive set of books and references. However, I believe it is useful and necessary to consult some of the works that relate specifically to the ideas involved in managing upwards. Hence this short booklist.

Back, K. and Back, K. (1990) *Assertiveness at Work*, Maidenhead: McGraw-Hill.

Blanchard, K., Oncken, W. and Burrows, H. (1990) *The One Minute Manager Meets the Monkey*, London: Fontana.

Coates, J. and Houchin, K. (1988) *Practical Management Development*, Alton: Nimrod Press.

Egan, G. (1993) *Adding Value*, Jossey-Bass (Management Series).

Handy, C. (1993) *Understanding Organizations*, London: Penguin.

Honey, P. and Mumford, A. (1986) *Using Your Learning Styles*, Maidenhead: Peter Honey.

Kotter, J. (1985) *Power and Influence*, New York: Free Press.

McCann, D. (1993) *How to Influence Others at Work*, London: Heinemann.

Mintzberg, H. and Quinn, J. B. (1991) *The Strategy Process: Concepts, Contexts, Cases*, London: Prentice Hall International.

Mumford, A. (1988) *Developing Top Managers*, Aldershot: Gower.

Mumford, A. (1986) *Learning to Learn for Managers*, Bradford: MCB University Press.

Stewart, R. (1982) *Choices for the Manager*, Maidenhead: McGraw-Hill.

Yasuda, Y. (1991) *40 Years: 20 Million Ideas*, Cambridge, MA: Productivity Press.

INDEX

Assertiveness for Managers

Terry Gillen

Flatter organizations, decentralized authority, changing technology, obsolete skills, downsizing, retraining, outplacement - these are common features of today's business environment. Against such a background, success depends increasingly on the personal credibility of individual managers. In this timely book, *Terry Gillen* explains how an assertive style of management can dramatically improve effectiveness. He sets out the principles and benefits of assertive behaviour and shows how to apply assertiveness techniques in everyday management situations.

Part One places assertiveness in the context of the modern manager's job, illustrates the three main types of behaviour and describes a method of harnessing emotional energy to ensure the desired results.

Part Two shows how to handle a range of management problems, including aggressive bosses or colleagues, receiving/giving criticism, disciplining staff, resolving conflict and controlling stress. Each chapter contains examples of the particular problem, guidance on how to deal with it assertively and a summary for rapid reference.

Contents

1992   257 pages   0 566 02861 1

Gower

Empowering People at Work

Nancy Foy

This is a book written, says the author, "for the benefit of practical managers coping with real people in real organizations". Part I shows how the elements of empowerment work together: performance focus, teams, leadership and face-to-face communication. Part II explains how to manage the process of empowerment, even in a climate of "downsizing" and "delayering". It includes chapters on networking, listening, running effective team meetings, giving feedback, training and using employee surveys. Part III contains case studies of IBM and British Telecom and examines the way they have developed employee communication to help achieve corporate objectives.

The final section comprises a review of communication channels that can be used to enhance the empowerment process, an extensive set of survey questions to be selected on a "pick and mix" basis and an annotated guide to further reading.

Empowerment is probably the most important concept in the world of management today, and Nancy Foy's new book will go a long way towards helping managers to "make it happen".

Contents

1994   288 pages   0 566 07436 2

Gower

Problem Solving in Groups

Second Edition

Mike Robson

Modern scientific research has demonstrated that groups are likely to solve problems more effectively than individuals. As most of us knew already, two heads (or more) are better than one. In organizations it makes sense to harness the power of the group both to deal with problems already identified and to generate ideas for enhancing effectiveness by reducing costs, increasing productivity and the like.

In this revised and updated edition of his successful book, Mike Robson first introduces the concepts and methods involved. Then, after setting out the advantages of the group approach, he examines in detail each of the eight key problem solving techniques. The final part of the book explains how to present proposed solutions, how to evaluate results and how to ensure that the group process runs smoothly.

With its practical tone, its down-to-earth style and lively visuals, this is a book that will appeal strongly to managers and trainers looking for ways of improving their organization's and their department's performance.

Contents

1993   176 pages   0 566 07414 1 Hardback   0 566 07415 X Paperback

Gower

Professional Report Writing

Simon Mort

Professional Report Writing is probably the most thorough treatment of this subject available, covering every aspect of an area often taken for granted. The author provides not just helpful analysis but also practical guidance on such topics as:

- deciding the format
- structuring a report
- stylistic pitfalls and how to avoid them
- making the most of illustrations
- ensuring a consistent layout

The theme throughout is fitness for purpose, and the text is enriched by a wide variety of examples drawn from the worlds of business, industry and government. The annotated bibliography includes a review of the leading dictionaries and reference books. Simon Mort's new book is destined to become an indispensable reference work for managers, civil servants, local government officers, consultants and professsionals of every kind.

Contents

Types and purposes of reports • Structure: introduction and body • Structure: conclusions and recommendations • Appendices and other attachments • Choosing words • Writing for non-technical readers • Style • Reviewing and editing • Summaries and concise writing • Visual illustrations • Preparing a report • Physical presentation • Appendix I Numbering systems • Appendix II Suggestions for further reading • Appendix III References • Index.

1992   232 pages   0 566 02712 7

Gower

Teambuilding Strategy

Mike Woodcock and Dave Francis

There is no doubt that working through teams can be an effective way to accomplish tasks in an organization. As Woodcock and Francis point out, though, it is by no means the only one. Managers concerned with human resource strategy cannot afford to assume that teamwork will always be the best option. A number of questions need to be asked before any decision is made, such as:

- what should be the focus of our organization development interventions?
- should we undertake teambuilding initiatives?
- how extensive should the teambuilding initiative be?
- what resources will we need to support our teambuilding initiative?

This book provides a framework within which these questions may be addressed. It presents a structured approach to analysing the key issues, including a series of questionnaires and activities designed to guide the reader through the key strategic decisions that must be taken by any organization contemplating a teambuilding programme. The authors, two of the best known specialists in the field, examine the benefits and dangers of teambuilding as an organization development strategy and offer detailed guidance on further information and resources.

This is the second and considerably reworked edition of *Organisation Development Through Teambuilding*, first published in 1982.

Contents

1994   160 pages   0 566 07496 6

Gower